LETTERS
WRITTEN DURING A SHORT RESIDENCE IN
SWEDEN, NORWAY, AND DENMARK

Mary Wollstonecraft

LETTERS

Written during a Short Residence in

Sweden, Norway, and Denmark

EDITED WITH AN INTRODUCTION BY
Carol H. Poston

UNIVERSITY OF NEBRASKA PRESS
LINCOLN & LONDON

Publishers on the Plains

UNP

Library of Congress Cataloging in Publication Data
Wollstonecraft, Mary, 1759–1797.
  Letters written during a short residence in Sweden, Norway, and
Denmark.

  Bibliography: p.
  1. Wollstonecraft, Mary, 1759–1797—Correspondence. 2. Imlay,
Gilbert, 1754?–1828? 3. Scandinavia—Description and travel. I. Title.
PR5841.W8Z53 1976   828'.6'09 [B]   75–38056
ISBN 0–8032–0862–6
ISBN 0–8032–5832–1 pbk.

CONTENTS

INTRODUCTION

ADMIRERS of Mary Wollstonecraft, foremost among whom was her husband William Godwin, have long insisted that her *Letters Written during a Short Residence in Sweden, Norway, and Denmark* (1796) is her most delightful work. And the gentle pace, brilliant observation, and moving passages on nature and self are the more amazing because this work, the last published in Wollstonecraft's lifetime, was written while she was undergoing great personal turmoil, a torment so grave that it had placed her on the brink of a principled attempt at suicide. The year the Scandinavian *Letters* were written, 1795, saw her imminent break-up with her lover Gilbert Imlay, as well as her distress over the political situation in France, from which she had just returned. Yet the *Letters* have a quality of mature self-knowledge and an appreciation of the world quite unlike the erratic brilliance of *A Vindication of the Rights of Woman* (1792) or the quivering indignation of her last, unfinished novel, *Maria, or the Wrongs of Woman.*

Fully understanding the *Letters* necessitates going back some three years before its composition. After the extraordinary success of *A Vindication of the Rights of Woman* had catapulted Wollstonecraft to fame, she decided to visit France, then undergoing a revolution, the principles of which she thoroughly supported. Her growing radicalism had been stated in the earlier *A Vindication of the Rights of Men* (1790), where she had castigated Edmund Burke for his conservative defense of the monarchy, the aristocracy, and the established Church in his *Reflections on the Revolution in France*. Like the Marxists in the twentieth century who held that Russia was not the best location for a communist revolution, Wollstonecraft, with her general contempt for French manners and morals, thought France not the most desirable amphitheater for the first victory of the rights of man—and woman. But nonetheless she desired to witness the political struggle firsthand, so in December of 1792 she sailed for the Continent.

Once in Paris she found herself in many ways quite alone because, although she knew written French well enough to have published translations, she found she was not articulate in spoken French. Nor had she anticipated the confusion she would feel about political events in France. In a letter to her publisher, Joseph Johnson, in December 1792, she confesses her emotion after watching the doomed Louis XVI carried by coach past her window on his way to his trial, and she says that "once or twice, lifting my eyes from the paper, I have seen eyes glare through a glass-door opposite my chair, and bloody hands shook at me.... I am going to bed—and, for the first time in my life, I cannot put out the candle."[1]

Wollstonecraft was soon rather amiably situated, however, in a group of Americans and English and French radicals in the capital. And it was in this social setting that she met Gilbert Imlay, an American author,

---

1. In *Posthumous Works*, ed. William Godwin (London, 1798), 4: 93–94.

explorer, and entrepreneur. He had fought in the American revolution and was the author both of a book about the topography and geography of Kentucky and a novel, *The Emigrants,* about to be published. It is not clear whether Wollstonecraft knew about Imlay's mission in Paris at the time, which seems to have been the raising of money and troops for a French military operation against the Spanish in the French-held colony of Louisiana. Nor in all likelihood did she correctly assess the character of the man with whom she had fallen in love, for Imlay, despite his initial devotion, was an inveterate Don Juan in impulse, and soon proved unfaithful. What he, on his part, had not perceived in regard to this particular flirtation was that he had attracted a woman of great intellect and of no small tenacity when it came to getting what she wanted; as Virginia Woolf described it, in "tickling minnows he had hooked a dolphin."[2]

By June of 1793, Wollstonecraft had moved to Neuilly, a nearby suburb of Paris where she felt she would be safer. In her retreat she worked on her history of the French Revolution (*A Historical and Moral View of the Origin and Progress of the French Revolution,* published by Joseph Johnson in 1794). In September she was registered as the wife of Gilbert Imlay at the American embassy, although the two were not married, because of the safety which would be afforded her as an American citizen (a status conferred on her automatically upon her marriage to an American). She was pregnant with their child when Imlay left for Le Havre later in 1793. He had become involved in the rather lucrative importing business, the military scheme against Louisi-

---

2. *The Second Common Reader* (New York: Harcourt Brace, 1932), p. 173.

ana having failed to get organized. Wollstonecraft's letters to Imlay during this period indicate that she did not approve of his "commercial" activities, nor had she changed her mind when she wrote the Scandinavian *Letters* some two years later (see Letter XXIII).

She followed her lover to Le Havre when he seemed to be unable to return to Paris for a visit, and there Fanny Imlay was born in 1794. While the mother revelled in her new daughter, the father returned to Paris and thence journeyed to London. Wollstonecraft and Fanny spent that long cold winter back in Paris. Only the delight in her nursing baby seemed to cheer her. Worries about her lover, concern about what to do should Imlay abandon them, and sporadic illness all combined to make the already grim French scene even more bleak. Challenged on its frontiers, collapsing from civil strife within, France had tried to restore order by force; but the crowded guillotine had not brought order either. Several months later in Sweden, looking at the verdant upland pastures enamelled with wild flowers, Wollstonecraft would say, "I gazed around with rapture, and felt more of that spontaneous pleasure which gives credibility to our expectation of happiness, than I had for a long, long time before. I forgot the horrors I had witnessed in France, which had cast a gloom over all nature" (Letter I).

In April 1795, Wollstonecraft, Fanny, and Marguerite, their French maid, arrived in London only to find Gilbert Imlay evasive and cold to all appeals to his domestic emotions. A few months previously he and Wollstonecraft had been planning to emigrate to America; only the requisite £1,000 in cash had been wanting, and the acquisition of money for the move is probably the only reason Mary Wollstonecraft had ever condoned Imlay's involvement in the shipping business in the first place. Wollstonecraft's biographers continue to speculate on the exact nature of the events after her reunion with Imlay in London, but it seems fairly certain that she knew her lover had forsaken her and that she was about to attempt suicide when he discovered her intention. In order to divert her—or possibly to distract her from his developing affair with another woman—Imlay hit upon the scheme of sending her to the Scandinavian countries as his business envoy. The journey was, then, a practical one, for while it was a business trip chiefly, it also at least permitted the possibility of Wollstonecraft's recovery, that is to say, her acceptance of their relationship upon Imlay's terms.

Wollstonecraft's chronicle of that summer of 1795 spent in the northern countries, in the form of letters written to Gilbert Imlay in London, was published in 1796 by Joseph Johnson as *Letters Written during a Short Residence in Sweden, Norway, and Denmark.* Wollstonecraft left Hull in June with one-year old Fanny and Marguerite, the nursemaid, in tow, and they returned via Hamburg and Dover the following September.

Because the letters were written to an actual person, they are lively and vivid, and for the most part avoid the artificiality that can sometimes be limiting in the epistolary form. They seem, moreover, not to have been edited very much or at all; personal apostrophe abounds, and in a couple of instances there are even phrases that can only be termed intimate. But by no means is the series of letters limited to personal topics, and Wollstonecraft's active mind, always overflowing, shows here at its finest. Indeed, it is possible that the epistolary journal is the perfect literary mode for Wollstonecraft's strengths as a writer and thinker, for in a journal an almost random movement from subject to subject is acceptable, even desirable. The most common complaint about *A Vindication of the Rights of Woman* centers on its alleged lack of unity; that work overflows with ideas and digressions which, perceptive as they are, often seem to get in the way of the book's chief argument. In the Scandinavian *Letters*, however, Wollstonecraft can with propriety range over an immense variety of subjects. It is this range from the personal to the universal, from social criticism to poetic reverie, and from personal apostrophe to abstract argumentation that makes the *Letters* so satisfying.

On one level the book is a journal of personal correspondence. On another it is an exercise in the familiar vein of eighteenth-century travel literature. Wollstonecraft had reviewed numerous travel books in her years at the *Analytical Review*, ranging from William Gilpin's country rambles to Jacques Brissot's North American *Travels* and J. G. Forster's diaries of the South Sea Islands. Wollstonecraft's allusions here to Laurence Sterne's *A Sentimental Journey* and probably to Johnson and Boswell's journey to the Hebrides, as well as her pronouncements on the most advantageous travel for young people and the virtues of journal keeping, all suggest that she was quite self-consciously posing as "the Traveller." But the *Letters* are also an interesting inversion of the epistolary travel literature of the period. The narrator is not embarked on a predictably important "Grand Tour"; rather she is journeying to a rarely-visited tip of the world. And the narrator is not only a female, which is rare enough, but she is travelling alone much of the time, a situation which puts her in constant concern at being overcharged for goods or services. When she does have companionship, it is that of an infant and a maid—unquestionably an unusual travelling party.

Wollstonecraft frequently alludes to the complications of travel, troubles which, in some measure, men also would have experienced; but there is no question that the problem was exacerbated for a single woman travelling with a child. There was always the problem of arranging conveyances, ordering post horses, and providing food for a long journey, as well as Marguerite's ever-present fear of "robberies, murders, or *the other evil*" (italics mine); there were unavoidable delays occasioned by uncooperative winds and unreasonable boat captains. All these, as well as Wollstonecraft's observation in Letter I that the Swedish mariner thought her an extraordinary woman because she asked "men's questions," serve to dramatize the uniqueness of the lone woman as a traveller.

Wollstonecraft, of course, was not simply a woman, but a woman with a practiced eye at observing the members of her own sex, and, by inclination, habituated to expressing herself at every opportunity about the wrongs suffered by women. So it is no surprise to find trenchant observations on the plight of females, the most cynical of which is her statement that, while servants in Sweden are generally ill-treated, still the males "stand up for the dignity of man by oppressing the women . . . . The most menial, and even laborious offices, are therefore left to these drudges" (Letter III). In the cold winter the women go down to the river to wash clothes in the icy water, and no self-respecting man would aid in this task even to the extent of carrying the heavy tubs. Wollstonecraft finds herself so often moralizing on the subject of women that at one point she says to Imlay, "Still harping on the same subject, you will exclaim—How can I avoid it, when most of the struggles of an eventful life have been occasioned by the oppressed state of my sex: we reason deeply, when we forcibly feel" (Letter XIX).

She extends her general feelings, of course, to her own daughter in particular. It is clear how she cherishes her "frolicker," her "Fannikin." Yet in Letter VI she laments to Imlay that their child is a girl, not because she does not love girls, but rather because some day her daughter may be "forced to sacrifice her heart to her principles, or principles to her heart." There is a grim propriety in her concluding phrase in the paragraph about little Fanny—"Hapless woman! what a fate is thine"—for twenty-one years later Fanny Imlay committed suicide in a Swansea hotel room chiefly out of despair at her love for the young Percy Bysshe Shelley.

Wollstonecraft is at once social critic, mother, and defender of the female sex when she descants on the virtues of clothing a child lightly and nursing one's baby oneself—neither of which practices is widespread in the countries she is visiting. And her zeal for the kind of dedicated motherhood usually suggested by nursing one's own child has its very practical side, for children sent out to country wet-nurses were more likely to perish of neglect or of tuberculosis or syphilis contracted from the nurse. It is the fact that syphilis is highly contagious that makes Wollstonecraft remark, in a passage that might otherwise be redolent of lofty moralizing, that "the total want of chastity in the lower class of women frequently renders them very unfit for the trust [of wet nurse]" (Letter IV).

The strength of the social criticism in this book is the strength of Mary Wollstonecraft: she does not stop being a woman or a mother or a political radical as she observes. She is always the social meliorist, looking about her for signs of "my favorite subject of contemplation, the future improvement of the world" (Letter XII). She even seems oddly gratified to note that the countries she is visiting are in many ways backward, because this fact affirms her belief in social evolution, the progress of humankind. She had explained her position in *A Vindication of the Rights of Woman:* "Rousseau exerts himself to prove that all *was* right originally: a crowd of authors that all *is* now right: and I, that all will *be* right."[3]

And of course here, as in her other work, the vehicle for social change is political equality and educational reform. The premise that all people should be treated as fully rational individuals, deserving of rights, underlies her fight for women's freedom as well as her argument for prison reform and her tolerance toward servants (she never progressed far enough to say that there need be no servants; they were always a given). Likewise a humane and sensible view of humanity fuels her arguments against capital punishment in Letter XIX, where she concludes that public executions, far from acting as a deterrent to crime, actually numb the viewers to murder, making them more callous and therefore more apt to commit crimes themselves. And finally, even her long-range view of humanity is revealed when, three years before T. A. Malthus's first published observations about the exponential increase in population and the geometric increase in food supply, Wollstonecraft in Letter XI is

---

3. Ed. Carol H. Poston (New York: Norton, 1976), p. 15.

concerned about "the state of man when the earth could no longer support him. Where was he to fly from universal famine?"

The *Letters* are rich with observations that jolt the present-day reader with their unexpected modernity: descriptions of the alum-making and canal-digging which ruin the appearance of the land, a highly skeptical view of the benefits of any organized religion, the essentially evolutionary position that it is the species, not the individual, which nature strives to protect. But social comment does not provide the real matrix of the *Letters*, widespread as is its occurrence. Rather, a quality of poetic reverie pervades and unifies the work. Wollstonecraft's deeply-felt emotions about nature keep recurring, and at the same time she soliloquizes about the nature of the universe and her place in it. There is a sense in which she shows an attitude toward nature and the self quite like Wordsworth's in "Lines Written a Few Miles above Tintern Abbey" when he describes his awareness of

> A motion and a spirit that impels
> All thinking things, all objects of all thought
> And rolls through all things.

But Wollstonecraft's feeling about nature is shaped by a dedication to science and reason characteristic of the Enlightenment. When she is tempted, for example, to look at herself as "a particle broken off from the grand mass of mankind," she uses a characteristic physical metaphor to complete her thought: "[then] some involuntary sympathetic emotion, like the attraction of adhesion, made me feel that I was still part of a mighty whole, from which I could not sever myself" (Letter I). Elsewhere, she responds to her natural environment in a fine reverie of cosmic consciousness, although the thought ends in a rather commonplace religious sentiment:

With what ineffable pleasure have I not gazed—and gazed again, losing my breath through my eyes—my very soul diffused itself in the scene—and, seeming to become all senses, glided in the scarcely agitated waves, melted in the freshening breeze . . . and, imperceptibly recalling the reveries of childhood, I bowed before the awful throne of my Creator, whilst I rested on its footstool (Letter VIII).

That her religious attitude toward nature suggests Wordsworth is perhaps only to say that Wollstonecraft has a world view and a background of reading quite like that of many Romantics. She was well-versed in those earlier authors who contributed to the Romantics' ability to look at nature in a new way. Her most constant descriptive word for the rocky beauty of Scandinavia is "sublime," used quite probably with Edmund Burke's definition in mind. Burke contrasts "sublime" and "beautiful": "sublime objects are vast in their dimensions, beautiful ones comparatively small; beauty should be smooth and polished; the great, rugged and negligent . . . beauty should not be obscure; the great ought to be dark and gloomy; beauty should be light and delicate; the great ought to be solid, and even massive."[4] The brooding seascapes and jutting coasts of the northern land inspire a sense of the sublime, according to Wollstonecraft, although "the sublime often [gives] place imperceptibly to the beautiful, dilating the emotions which were painfully concentrated." When she does describe tranquil settings and arranged beauty, the word "pic-

---

4. *A Philosophical Enquiry into the Origin of Our Ideas of the Sublime and the Beautiful* (London, 1797 [rpt. Menston, England: The Scolar Press, Ltd., 1970]), pp. 237–38.

turesque" often occurs. Given a special currency by William Gilpin, whose *Wye Tour, Lakes Tour,* and *Scottish Tour* Wollstonecraft had read and reviewed for the *Analytical Review,* the term "picturesque" refers to that felicitous arrangement of natural beauty which, in its perfection, presents a veritable picture to the beholder. The picturesque often includes people, animals, or buildings to fill out the canvas, whereas the sublime nearly always is composed of vast and impressive objects in nature.

In Burke, the "sublime" is extended to works of art as well as to objects in nature. Perhaps related to Burke's aesthetic as well as to her own preoccupation with death, one motif in the *Letters* is the sublime as applied not only to the landscape, but to the human soul. Wollstonecraft dwells on death, not always morbidly, but rather as "something getting free"; her idea of eternity is not the conventional one, but that which she sees in the cascade, "the always varying, still the same, torrent before me—I stretched out my hand to eternity, bounding over the dark speck of life to come." The *Letters* are replete with quotations from *King Lear, Hamlet,* and *Macbeth.* As she walks over the ashes of the fires in Copenhagen she finds herself reflecting that she walks on the dead, and she comments that "they suffered—but they are no more!" As she listens to the cries of her hungry child on a sea crossing, she thinks of the death of Ugolino, who perished of starvation, locked in a tower with sons and grandsons. And as she says farewell to travelling companions, she speaks of separation as "a most melancholy, death-like idea." The great silence in Denmark is "death-like . . . where every house made me think of a tomb." She is on the verge of measuring herself against the universe and of calculating an idea of eternity. "Life," she writes, "what art thou? Where goes this breath? this *I*, so much alive? In what element will it mix, giving or receiving fresh energy?—What will break the enchantment of animation?" And then, with a doubt that must have warmed William Godwin's heart, she observes that the mummies she has just seen will require some considerable repair before they join the angels on the "day of judgment, if there is to be such a day" (Letter VII).

It must be said that our knowledge of what was to befall Mary Wollstonecraft in her immediate future often renders these thoughts and words written in 1795 even more poignant. In a few months' time she attempted suicide by a leap off Putney Bridge and, having fallen unconscious in the water, was rescued by some Thames boatmen. Painfully and gradually she conquered her passion for Gilbert Imlay and tried to build a new life, one likely to be productive and even tranquil, though all too brief. Her marriage to William Godwin in 1797, the anticipation of a life embracing domesticity and reading and writing, the delight of another baby to be cherished as fully as "Fannikin," finally gave her a new zest for life—just when that vibrant life ended. When reading her evocative cry of anguish in Letter VIII, one must think of her untimely death shortly after the birth of her second daughter Mary just two years later:

I cannot bear to think of being no more—of losing myself—though existence is often but a painful consciousness of misery; nay it appears to me impossible that I should cease to exist, or that this active, restless spirit, equally alive to joy or sorrow, should only be organized dust—ready to fly abroad the moment the spring snaps, or the spark goes out, which kept it together.

This passage summarizes what is ceaselessly gripping about Mary Wollstonecraft: she argued and lived and wrote with an intensity and a vision born of personal experience yet informed by a larger social and aesthetic reality. A wealth of ideas, years of wide reading, and a restless and observant eye make her *Letters Written during a Short Residence in Sweden, Norway, and Denmark* quite possibly the perfect fusion of the personal and intellectual selves of Mary Wollstonecraft.

Note on the Text

In the preparation of this edition I have been careful to preserve the work of Mary Wollstonecraft as it was printed in the only English text which ever appeared, Joseph Johnson's 1796 edition. Because the text has not been "improved," the reader will note eccentric and inconsistent spelling and haphazard punctuation. I have regularized the capitalization of the names of cities, countries, and days of the week (which are inconsistently capitalized in the original), so that the text will read more smoothly. Wollstonecraft's use of lower case has been allowed purposely to remain in words referring to religious sects; such words are regularly lower-cased in the text save the single instance of "Lutherans" on page 45, and it is possible that, because of her dissatisfaction with organized religion, the lower-case denomination was requested by Wollstonecraft. The text has been changed in four places for sense: "aud" has been made "and" on page 23, line 3; "inhaste" has been made into two words on page 48, line 4; a comma has been substituted for the dash after "peasant" on page 114, line 1; and an "and" has been added before "of course" to the third sentence on page 148. The only changes I have made are in matters of printers' conventions (a change of occasional single quotation marks to double marks, for example) that in no way affect the sense or rhythm of the text.

My notes, which appear along with Wollstonecraft's original notes as footnotes at the bottom of appropriate pages, are designed to identify quotations and clarify allusions. And a map has been provided to show Wollstonecraft's itinerary.

SELECTED BIBLIOGRAPHY

All of Mary Wollstonecraft's works are now available to the modern reader in either facsimile or modern reprint versions; and an extensive bibliography, annotated modern editions of some of the works, and all of the letters are either now or soon will be available. Listed below is a selected group of books and articles on Wollstonecraft which should be useful for the reader interested in further study.

Benedict, Ruth. *An Anthropologist at Work*, ed. Margaret Mead. Boston: Houghton-Mifflin, 1959.

Bouten, Jacob. *Mary Wollstonecraft and the Beginnings of Female Emancipation in France and England.* Amsterdam: H. J. Paris, 1922.

Flexner, Eleanor. *Mary Wollstonecraft.* New York: Coward, McCann, Geoghegan, 1972.

George, Margaret. *One Woman's Situation: A Study of Mary Wollstonecraft.* Urbana: University of Illinois Press, 1970.

Godwin, William. *Memoirs of the Author of "A Vindication of the Rights of Woman."* London: Joseph Johnson, 1798.

Linford, Madeleine. *Mary Wollstonecraft (1759–1797).* London: Leonard Parsons, 1924.

Norman, Sylvia. Introduction to Mary Wollstonecraft, *Letters Written during a Short Residence in Sweden, Norway, and Denmark*. Fontwell, Sussex: Centaur Press, 1970. [Facsimile edition.]

Paul, Charles Kegan. *William Godwin: His Friends and Contemporaries*. Boston: Roberts Brothers, 1876.

Pennell, Elizabeth Robins. *Mary Wollstonecraft Godwin*. London: W. H. Allen and Co., 1885.

Preedy, George R. [Pseudonym for Mrs. Gabrielle Campbell Long]. *This Shining Woman*. London: Collins, 1937.

Rauschenbusch-Clough, Emma. *A Study of Mary Wollstonecraft and the Rights of Woman*. London: Longmans, Green, and Co., 1898.

Roper, Derek. "Mary Wollstonecraft's Reviews." *Notes and Queries*, 5 (January, 1958): 37–38.

Taylor, G. R. S. *Mary Wollstonecraft: A Study in Economics and Romance*. London: Martin Secker, 1911.

Tomalin, Claire. *The Life and Death of Mary Wollstonecraft*. New York and London: Harcourt Brace Jovanovich, 1974.

Wardle, R. M. "Mary Wollstonecraft, *Analytical* Reviewer." *PMLA*, 62 (December, 1947): 1000–1009.

_____. *Mary Wollstonecraft: A Critical Biography*. Lawrence: University of Kansas Press, 1951.

LETTERS

WRITTEN

DURING A SHORT RESIDENCE

IN

SWEDEN, NORWAY, AND DENMARK.

BY MARY WOLLSTONECRAFT.

LONDON:
PRINTED FOR J. JOHNSON, ST. PAUL'S CHURCH-YARD.

1796.

WOLLSTONECRAFT'S
SCANDINAVIAN ITINERARY

The place-name spellings used here and on the facing map are Wollstonecraft's; the names in parentheses are the spellings as found in the current London *Times* Atlas of the World.

[Hull, England]; unnamed island off the coast of Sweden; Gothenburg (Göteborg), Sweden; Quistram (Kvistram), Sweden; Stromstad (Strömstad), Sweden; Fredericshall (Halden), Norway; return to Stromstad, Sweden; Laurvig (Larvik), Norway; Tonsberg (Tönsberg), Norway, on July 17, where she stays three weeks; return to Laurvig, Norway; briefly at Helgeraac (Helgeroa), Norway; driven by weather and darkness to Portoer (Portöy), Norway; Rusoer (Risör), Norway; return to Helgeraac, Norway; return to Tonsberg, Norway; Moss, Norway; Christiania (Oslo), Norway; Fredericstadt (Frederikstad), Norway, where she visits a nearby cataract; return to Stromstad, Sweden; stops at Quistram en route to Uddervalla (Uddevalla), Sweden; Gothenburg, Sweden; a side trip to see the cascade at Trolhaettae (Trolhätte), Sweden; return to Gothenburg; Falckersberg (Falkenberg), Sweden; Elsineur (Helsingør), Denmark; Copenhagen (København), Denmark; Corsoer (Korsør), Denmark; Sleswick (Schleswig, then under Danish control), Germany; passes through Itzchol (Itzehoe), Germany; Hamburg, Germany, but has her lodgings in nearby Altona; [Dover, England]

ADVERTISEMENT

THE WRITING travels, or memoirs, has ever been a pleasant employment; for vanity or sensibility always renders it interesting. In writing these desultory letters, I found I could not avoid being continually the first person—"the little hero of each tale." I tried to correct this fault, if it be one, for they were designed for publication; but in proportion as I arranged my thoughts, my letter, I found, became stiff and affected: I, therefore, determined to let my remarks and reflections flow unrestrained, as I perceived that I could not give a just description of what I saw, but by relating the effect different objects had produced on my mind and feelings, whilst the impression was still fresh.

A person has a right, I have sometimes thought, when amused by a witty or interesting egotist, to talk of himself when he can win on our attention by acquiring our affection. Whether I deserve to rank amongst this privileged number, my readers alone can judge—and I give them leave to shut the book, if they do not wish to become better acquainted with me.

My plan was simply to endeavour to give a just view of the present state of the countries I have passed through, as far as I could obtain information during so short a residence; avoiding those details which, without being very useful to travellers who follow the same route, appear very insipid to those who only accompany you in their chair.

LETTER I

ELEVEN days of weariness on board a vessel not intended for the accommodation of passengers have so
exhausted my spirits, to say nothing of the other causes,
with which you are already sufficiently acquainted, that
it is with some difficulty I adhere to my determination
of giving you my observations, as I travel through new
scenes, whilst warmed with the impression they have
made on me.

The captain, as I mentioned to you, promised to put
me on shore at Arendall,[1] or Gothenburg, in his way to
Elsineur; but contrary winds obliged us to pass both
places during the night. In the morning, however, after
we had lost sight of the entrance of the latter bay, the
vessel was becalmed; and the captain, to oblige me,
hanging out a signal for a pilot, bore down towards the
shore.

My attention was particularly directed to the light-
house; and you can scarcely imagine with what anxiety
I watched two long hours for a boat to emancipate me
—still no one appeared. Every cloud that flitted on the
horizon was hailed as a liberator, till approaching

---

1. In Norway. [Author's note.]

nearer, like most of the prospects sketched by hope, it dissolved under the eye into disappointment.

Weary of expectation, I then began to converse with the captain on the subject; and, from the tenour of the information my questions drew forth, I soon concluded, that, if I waited for a boat, I had little chance of getting on shore at this place. Despotism, as is usually the case, I found had here cramped the industry of man. The pilots being paid by the king, and scantily, they will not run into any danger, or even quit their hovels, if they can possibly avoid it, only to fulfil what is termed their duty. How different is it on the English coast, where, in the most stormy weather, boats immediately hail you, brought out by the expectation of extraordinary profit.

Disliking to sail for Elsineur, and still more to lie at anchor, or cruise about the coast for several days, I exerted all my rhetoric to prevail on the captain to let me have the ship's boat; and though I added the most forcible of arguments, I for a long time addressed him in vain.

It is a kind of rule at sea, not to send out a boat. The captain was a good-natured man; but men with common minds seldom break through general rules. Prudence is ever the resort of weakness; and they rarely go as far as they may in any undertaking, who are determined not to go beyond it on any account. If, however, I had some trouble with the captain, I did not lose much time with the sailors; for they, all alacrity, hoisted out the boat, the moment I obtained permission, and promised to row me to the light-house.

I did not once allow myself to doubt of obtaining a conveyance from thence round the rocks—and then away for Gothenburg—confinement is so unpleasant.

LETTER I

The day was fine; and I enjoyed the water till, approaching the little island, poor Marguerite, whose timidity always acts as a feeler before her adventuring spirit, began to wonder at our not seeing any inhabitants. I did not listen to her. But when, on landing, the same silence prevailed, I caught the alarm, which was not lessened by the sight of two old men, whom we forced out of their wretched hut. Scarcely human in their appearance, we with difficulty obtained an intelligible reply to our questions—the result of which was, that they had no boat, and were not allowed to quit their post, on any pretence. But, they informed us, that there was at the other side, eight or ten miles over, a pilot's dwelling; two guineas tempted the sailors to risk the captain's displeasure, and once more embark to row me over.

The weather was pleasant, and the appearance of the shore so grand, that I should have enjoyed the two hours it took to reach it, but for the fatigue which was too visible in the countenances of the sailors who, instead of uttering a complaint, were, with the thoughtless hilarity peculiar to them, joking about the possibility of the captain's taking advantage of a slight westerly breeze, which was springing up, to sail without them. Yet, in spite of their good humour, I could not help growing uneasy when the shore, receding, as it were, as we advanced, seemed to promise no end to their toil. This anxiety increased when, turning into the most picturesque bay I ever saw, my eyes sought in vain for the vestige of a human habitation. Before I could determine what step to take in such a dilemma, for I could not bear to think of returning to the ship, the sight of a barge relieved me, and we hastened towards it for information. We were immediately directed to pass some jutting rocks when we should see a pilot's hut.

There was a solemn silence in this scene, which made itself be felt. The sun-beams that played on the ocean, scarcely ruffled by the lightest breeze, contrasted with the huge, dark rocks, that looked like the rude materials of creation forming the barrier of unwrought space, forcibly struck me; but I should not have been sorry if the cottage had not appeared equally tranquil. Approaching a retreat where strangers, especially women, so seldom appeared, I wondered that curiosity did not bring the beings who inhabited it to the windows or door. I did not immediately recollect that men who remain so near the brute creation, as only to exert themselves to find the food necessary to sustain life, have little or no imagination to call forth the curiosity necessary to fructify the faint glimmerings of mind which entitles them to rank as lords of the creation. —Had they either, they could not contentedly remain rooted in the clods they so indolently cultivate.

Whilst the sailors went to seek for the sluggish inhabitants, these conclusions occurred to me; and, recollecting the extreme fondness which the Parisians ever testify for novelty, their very curiosity appeared to me a proof of the progress they had made in refinement. Yes; in the art of living—in the art of escaping from the cares which embarrass the first steps towards the attainment of the pleasures of social life.

The pilots informed the sailors that they were under the direction of a lieutenant retired from the service, who spoke English; adding, that they could do nothing without his orders; and even the offer of money could hardly conquer their laziness, and prevail on them to accompany us to his dwelling. They would not go with me alone which I wanted them to have done, because I wished to dismiss the sailors as soon as possible. Once more we rowed off, they following tardily, till, turning round another bold protuberance of the rocks, we saw a boat making towards us, and soon learnt that it was the lieutenant himself, coming with some earnestness to see who we were.

To save the sailors any further toil, I had my baggage instantly removed into his boat; for, as he could speak English, a previous parley was not necessary; though Marguerite's respect for me could hardly keep her from expressing the fear, strongly marked on her countenance, which my putting ourselves into the power of a strange man excited. He pointed out his cottage; and, drawing near to it, I was not sorry to see a female figure, though I had not, like Marguerite, been thinking of robberies, murders, or the other evil which instantly, as the sailors would have said, runs foul of a woman's imagination.

On entering, I was still better pleased to find a clean house, with some degree of rural elegance. The beds were of muslin, coarse it is true, but dazzlingly white; and the floor was strewed over with little sprigs of juniper (the custom, as I afterwards found, of the country), which formed a contrast with the curtains and produced an agreeable sensation of freshness, to soften the ardour of noon. Still nothing was so pleasing as the alacrity of hospitality—all that the house afforded was quickly spread on the whitest linen. —Remember I had just left the vessel, where, without being fastidious, I had continually been disgusted. Fish, milk, butter, and cheese, and I am sorry to add, brandy, the bane of this country, were spread on the board. After we had dined, hospitality made them, with some degree of mystery, bring us some excellent coffee. I did not then know that it was prohibited.[2]

The good man of the house apologized for coming in continually, but declared that he was so glad to speak English, he could not stay out. He need not have apologized; I was equally glad of his company. With the wife I could only exchange smiles; and she was employed observing the make of our clothes. My hands, I found, had first led her to discover that I was the lady. I had, of course, my quantum of reverences; for the politeness of the north seems to partake of the coldness of the climate, and the rigidity of its iron sinewed rocks. Amongst the peasantry, there is, however, so much of the simplicity of the golden age[3] in this land of flint—so much overflowing of heart, and fellow-feeling, that only benevolence, and the honest sympathy of nature, diffused smiles over my countenance when they kept me standing, regardless of my fatigue, whilst they dropt courtesy after courtesy.

The situation of this house was beautiful, though chosen for convenience. The master being the officer who commanded all the pilots on the coast, and the person appointed to guard wrecks, it was necessary for him to fix on a spot that would overlook the whole bay. As he had seen some service, he wore, not without a pride I thought becoming, a badge to prove that he had

---

2. The sumptuary laws at the time forbade the import or use of coffee.

3. Though the idea of a "golden age"—a mythical primordial state of humankind characterized by happiness and freedom from sin and evil—originated with the Greek and Latin poets, it had considerable intellectual currency during the eighteenth century.

merited well of his country. It was happy, I thought, that he had been paid in honour; for the stipend he received was little more than twelve pounds a year. — I do not trouble myself or you with the calculation of Swedish ducats. Thus, my friend, you perceive the necessity of *perquisites.*[4] This same narrow policy runs through every thing. I shall have occasion further to animadvert on it.

Though my host amused me with an account of himself, which gave me an idea of the manners of the people I was about to visit, I was eager to climb the rocks to view the country, and see whether the honest tars had regained their ship. With the help of the lieutenant's telescope I saw the vessel underway with a fair though gentle gale. The sea was calm, playful even as the most shallow stream, and on the vast bason[5] I did not see a dark speck to indicate the boat. My conductors were consequently arrived.

Straying further, my eye was attracted by the sight of some heart's-ease[6] that peeped through the rocks. I caught at it as a good omen, and going to preserve it in a letter that had not conveyed balm to my heart, a cruel remembrance suffused my eyes; but it passed away like an April shower. If you are deep read in Shakspeare, you will recollect that this was the little western flower tinged by love's dart, which "maidens call love in idle-

---

4. Emoluments in addition to salary; the suggestion here is that the lieutenant, because of his scanty wages, gets money from other sources such as, perhaps, smuggling. See the author's discussion of the subject on pages 86–87. See also p. 99.

5. A common spelling for "basin."

6. A small wildflower, probably a wild pansy.

ness."[7] The gaiety of my babe was unmixed; regardless of omens or sentiments, she found a few wild strawberries more grateful than flowers or fancies.

The lieutenant informed me that this was a commodious bay. Of that I could not judge, though I felt its picturesque beauty. Rocks were piled on rocks, forming a suitable bulwark to the ocean. Come no further, they emphatically said, turning their dark sides to the waves to augment the idle roar. The view was sterile: still little patches of earth, of the most exquisite verdure, enamelled with the sweetest wild flowers, seemed to promise the goats and a few straggling cows luxurious herbage. How silent and peaceful was the scene. I gazed around with rapture, and felt more of that spontaneous pleasure which gives credibility to our expectation of happiness, than I had for a long, long time before. I forgot the horrors I had witnessed in France, which had cast a gloom over all nature, and suffering the enthusiasm of my character, too often, gracious God! damped by the tears of disappointed affection, to be lighted up afresh, care took wing while simple fellow feeling expanded my heart.

To prolong this enjoyment, I readily assented to the proposal of our host to pay a visit to a family, the master of which spoke English, who was the drollest dog in the country, he added, repeating some of his stories, with a hearty laugh.

I walked on, still delighted with the rude beauties of the scene; for the sublime often gave place imperceptibly to the beautiful, dilating the emotions which were painfully concentrated.

---

7. *Midsummer Night's Dream*, II.i.168; Oberon put the juice from this flower ("love-in-idleness") into Titania's eyes.

When we entered this abode, the largest I had yet seen, I was introduced to a numerous family; but the father, from whom I was led to expect so much entertainment, was absent. The lieutenant consequently was obliged to be the interpreter of our reciprocal compliments. The phrases were awkwardly transmitted, it is true; but looks and gestures were sufficient to make them intelligible and interesting. The girls were all vivacity, and respect for me could scarcely keep them from romping with my host, who, asking for a pinch of snuff, was presented with a box, out of which an artificial mouse, fastened to the bottom, sprung. Though this trick had doubtless been played time out of mind, yet the laughter it excited was not less genuine.

They were overflowing with civility; but to prevent their almost killing my babe with kindness, I was obliged to shorten my visit; and two or three of the girls accompanied us, bringing with them a part of whatever the house afforded to contribute towards rendering my supper more plentiful; and plentiful in fact it was, though I with difficulty did honour to some of the dishes, not relishing the quantity of sugar and spices put into every thing. At supper my host told me bluntly that I was a woman of observation, for I asked him *men's questions.*

The arrangements for my journey were quickly made; I could only have a car with post-horses, as I did not chuse to wait till a carriage could be sent for to Gothenburg. The expense of my journey, about one or two and twenty English miles, I found would not amount to more than eleven or twelve shillings, paying, he assured me, generously. I gave him a guinea and a half. But it was with the greatest difficulty that I could make him take so much, indeed any thing for my lodging and fare. He declared that it was next to robbing me, explaining how much I ought to pay on the road. However, as I was positive, he took the guinea for himself; but, as a condition, insisted on accompanying me, to prevent my meeting with any trouble or imposition on the way.

I then retired to my apartment with regret. The night was so fine, that I would gladly have rambled about much longer; yet recollecting that I must rise very early, I reluctantly went to bed: but my senses had been so awake, and my imaginagion still continued so busy, that I sought for rest in vain. Rising before six, I scented the sweet morning air; I had long before heard the birds twittering to hail the dawning day, though it could scarcely have been allowed to have departed.

Nothing, in fact, can equal the beauty of the northern summer's evening and night; if night it may be called that only wants the glare of day, the full light, which frequently seems so impertinent; for I could write at midnight very well without a candle. I contemplated all nature at rest; the rocks, even grown darker in their appearance, looked as if they partook of the general repose, and reclined more heavily on their foundation. —What, I exclaimed, is this active principle which keeps me still awake? —Why fly my thoughts abroad when every thing around me appears at home? My child was sleeping with equal calmness—innocent and sweet as the closing flowers. —Some recollections, attached to the idea of home, mingled with reflections respecting the state of society I had been contemplating that evening, made a tear drop on the rosy cheek I had just kissed; and emotions that trembled on the brink of extacy and agony gave a poignancy to my sensations, which made me feel more alive than usual.

LETTER I

What are these imperious sympathies? How frequently has melancholy and even mysanthropy taken possession of me, when the world has disgusted me, and friends have proved unkind. I have then considered myself as a particle broken off from the grand mass of mankind;—I was alone, till some involuntary sympathetic emotion, like the attraction of adhesion, made me feel that I was still a part of a mighty whole, from which I could not sever myself—not, perhaps, for the reflection has been carried very far, by snapping the thread of an existence which loses its charms in proportion as the cruel experience of life stops or poisons the current of the heart. Futurity, what hast thou not to give to those who know that there is such a thing as happiness! I speak not of philosophical contentment, though pain has afforded them the strongest conviction of it.

After our coffee and milk, for the mistress of the house had been roused long before us by her hospitality, my baggage was taken forward in a boat by my host, because the car could not safely have been brought to the house.

The road at first was very rocky and troublesome; but our driver was careful, and the horses accustomed to the frequent and sudden acclivities and descents; so that not apprehending any danger, I played with my girl, whom I would not leave to Marguerite's care, on account of her timidity.

Stopping at a little inn to bait the horses, I saw the first countenance in Sweden that displeased me, though the man was better dressed than any one who had as yet fallen in my way. An altercation took place between him and my host, the purport of which I could not guess, excepting that I was the occasion of it, be it what it would. The sequel was his leaving the house angrily; and I was immediately informed that he was the custom-house officer. The professional had indeed effaced the national character, for living as he did with these frank hospitable people, still only the exciseman appeared,—the counterpart of some I had met with in England and France. I was unprovided with a passport, not having entered any great town. At Gothenburg I knew I could immediately obtain one, and only the trouble made me object to the searching my trunks. He blustered for money; but the lieutenant was determined to guard me, according to promise, from imposition.

To avoid being interrogated at the town-gate, and obliged to go in the rain to give an account of myself, merely a form, before we could get the refreshment we stood in need of, he requested us to descend, I might have said step, from our car, and walk into town.

I expected to have found a tolerable inn, but was ushered into a most comfortless one; and, because it was about five o'clock, three or four hours after their dining hour, I could not prevail on them to give me any thing warm to eat.

The appearance of the accommodations obliged me to deliver one of my recommendatory letters, and the gentleman, to whom it was addressed, sent to look out for a lodging for me whilst I partook of his supper. As nothing passed at this supper to characterize the country, I shall here close my letter.

Your's truly.

LETTER II

GOTHENBURG is a clean airy town, and having been
built by the Dutch, has canals running through each
street,[1] and in some of them there are rows of trees that
would render it very pleasant were it not for the pavement, which is intolerably bad.

There are several rich commercial houses, Scotch,
French, and Swedish; but the Scotch, I believe, have
been the most successful. The commerce and commission business with France since the war,[2] has been very
lucrative, and enriched the merchants, I am afraid, at
the expence of the other inhabitants, by raising the
price of the necessaries of life.

As all the men of consequence, I mean men of the
largest fortune, are merchants, their principal enjoyment is a relaxation from business at the table, which is
spread at, I think, too early an hour (between one and
two) for men who have letters to write and accounts to

---

1. The canals in Gothenburg had been constructed in the early seventeenth century by the Lowland settlers, the Walloons.

2. After the Battle of Svenskund in 1790, Sweden's King Gustavus III
had signed a peace treaty with Russia; he was assassinated in 1792 at a
masked ball at the Opera House, and, though internal confusion followed,
the country had declared no new wars.

settle after paying due respect to the bottle. However, when numerous circles are to be brought together, and when neither literature nor public amusements furnish topics for conversation, a good dinner appears to be the only centre to rally round, especially as scandal, the zest of more select parties, can only be whispered. As for politics, I have seldom found it a subject of continual discussion in a country town in any part of the world. The politics of the place being on a smaller scale, suits better with the size of their faculties; for, generally speaking, the sphere of observation determines the extent of the mind.

The more I see of the world, the more I am convinced that civilization is a blessing not sufficiently estimated by those who have not traced its progress; for it not only refines our enjoyments, but produces a variety which enables us to retain the primitive delicacy of our sensations. Without the aid of the imagination all the pleasures of the senses must sink into grossness, unless continual novelty serve as a substitute for the imagination, which being impossible, it was to this weariness, I suppose, that Solomon alluded when he declared that there was nothing new under the sun![3]—nothing for the common sensations excited by the senses. Yet who will deny that the imagination and understanding have made many, very many discoveries since those days, which only seem harbingers of others still more noble and beneficial. I never met with much imagination amongst people who had not acquired a habit of reflection; and in that state of society in which the judgment and taste are not called forth, and formed by the cultivation of the arts and sciences, little of that delicacy of feeling

3. Ecclesiastes 1:9.

and thinking is to be found characterized by the word sentiment. The want of scientific pursuits perhaps accounts for the hospitality, as well as for the cordial reception which strangers receive from the inhabitants of small towns.

Hospitality has, I think, been too much praised by travellers as a proof of goodness of heart, when in my opinion indiscriminate hospitality is rather a criterion by which you may form a tolerable estimate of the indolence or vacancy of a head; or, in other words, a fondness for social pleasures in which the mind not having its proportion of exercise, the bottle must be pushed about.

These remarks are equally applicable to Dublin, the most hospitable city I ever passed through.[4] But I will try to confine my observations more particularly to Sweden.

It is true I have only had a glance over a small part of it; yet of its present state of manners and acquirements I think I have formed a distinct idea, without having visited the capital, where, in fact, less of a national character is to be found than in the remote parts of the country.

The Swedes pique themselves on their politeness; but far from being the polish of a cultivated mind, it consists merely of tiresome forms and ceremonies. So far indeed from entering immediately into your character, and making you feel instantly at your ease, like the well-bred French, their over-acted civility is a continual restraint on all your actions. The sort of superiority which a fortune gives when there is no superiority of

---

4. Wollstonecraft had spent time in Dublin in 1787 when she was a governess in the employ of Lord and Lady Kingsborough of County Cork.

education, excepting what consists in the observance of
senseless forms, has a contrary effect than what is intended; so that I could not help reckoning the peasantry
the politest people of Sweden, who only aiming at
pleasing you, never think of being admired for their
behaviour.

Their tables, like their compliments, seem equally a
caricature of the French. The dishes are composed, as
well as theirs, of a variety of mixtures to destroy the
native taste of the food without being as relishing.
Spices and sugar are put into every thing, even into the
bread; and the only way I can account for their partial-
ity to high-seasoned dishes, is the constant use of salted
provisions. Necessity obliges them to lay up a store of
dried fish, and salted meat, for the winter; and in summer, fresh meat and fish taste insipid after them. To
which may be added the constant use of spirits. Every
day, before dinner and supper, even whilst the dishes
are cooling on the table, men and women repair to a
side-table, and to obtain an appetite, eat bread and butter, cheese, raw salmon, or anchovies, drinking a glass
of brandy. Salt fish or meat then immediately follows,
to give a further whet to the stomach. As the dinner
advances, pardon me for taking up a few minutes to
describe what, alas! has detained me two or three hours
on the stretch, observing, dish after dish is changed, in
endless rotation, and handed round with solemn pace to
each guest: but should you happen not to like the first
dishes, which was often my case, it is a gross breach of
politeness to ask for part of any other till its turn comes.
But have patience, and there will be eating enough.
Allow me to run over the acts of a visiting day, not
overlooking the interludes.

LETTER II

Prelude a luncheon—then a succession of fish, flesh and fowl for two hours; during which time the desert, I was sorry for the strawberries and cream, rests on the table to be impregnated by the fumes of the viands. Coffee immediately follows in the drawing-room; but does not preclude punch, ale, tea and cakes, raw salmon, &c. A supper brings up the rear, not forgetting the introductory luncheon, almost equalling in removes the dinner. A day of this kind you would imagine sufficient —but a to-morrow and a to-morrow—A never ending, still beginning feast may be bearable, perhaps, when stern winter frowns, shaking with chilling aspect his hoary locks; but during a summer, sweet as fleeting, let me, my kind strangers, escape sometimes into your fir groves, wander on the margin of your beautiful lakes, or climb your rocks to view still others in endless perspective; which, piled by more than giant's hand, scale the heavens[5] to intercept its rays, or to receive the parting tinge of lingering day—day that, scarcely softened into twilight, allows the freshening breeze to wake, and the moon to burst forth in all her glory to glide with solemn elegance through the azure expanse.

The cow's bell has ceased to tinkle the herd to rest; they have all paced across the heath. Is not this the witching time of night? The waters murmur, and fall with more than mortal music, and spirits of peace walk abroad to calm the agitated breast. Eternity is in these moments: worldly cares melt into the airy stuff that

---

5. See Milton's *Paradise Lost*, IV.354–55: "and in th' ascending Scale/ Of Heav'n the Stars that usher Evening rose."

dreams are made of;[6] and reveries, mild and enchanting
as the first hopes of love, or the recollection of lost
enjoyment, carry the hapless wight into futurity, who,
in bustling life, has vainly strove to throw off the grief
which lies heavy at the heart. Good night! A crescent
hangs out in the vault before, which woos me to stray
abroad: —it is not a silvery reflection of the sun, but
glows with all its golden splendour. Who fears the falling dew? It only makes the mown grass smell more
fragrant.

Adieu!

---

6. *The Tempest*, IV .i. 156–57: "We are such stuff / As dreams are made
on . . .".

LETTER III

THE POPULATION of Sweden has been estimated from two millions and a half to three millions; a small number for such an immense tract of country: of which only so much is cultivated, and that in the simplest manner, as is absolutely necessary to supply the necessaries of life; and near the seashore, from whence herrings are easily procured, there scarcely appears a vestige of cultivation. The scattered huts that stand shivering on the naked rocks, braving the pitiless elements, are formed of logs of wood, rudely hewn; and so little pains are taken with the craggy foundation, that nothing like a pathway points out the door.

Gathered into himself by the cold, lowering his visage to avoid the cutting blast, is it surprising that the churlish pleasure of drinking drams takes place of social enjoyments amongst the poor, especially if we take into the account, that they mostly live on high-seasoned provisions and rye bread? Hard enough, you may imagine, as it is only baked once a year. The servants also, in most families, eat this kind of bread, and have a different kind of food from their masters, which, in spite of all the arguments I have heard to vindicate the custom, appears to me a remnant of barbarism.

In fact, the situation of the servants in every respect, particularly that of the women, shews how far the Swedes are from having a just conception of rational equality. They are not *termed* slaves; yet a man may strike a man with impunity because he pays him wages; though these wages are so low, that necessity must teach them to pilfer, whilst servility renders them false and boorish. Still the men stand up for the dignity of man, by oppressing the women. The most menial, and even laborious offices, are therefore left to these poor drudges. Much of this I have seen. In the winter, I am told, they take the linen down to the river, to wash it in the cold water; and though their hands, cut by the ice, are cracked and bleeding, the men, their fellow servants, will not disgrace their manhood by carrying a tub to lighten their burden.

You will not be surprised to hear that they do not wear shoes or stockings, when I inform you that their wages are seldom more than twenty or thirty shillings per annum. It is the custom, I know, to give them a new year's gift, and a present at some other period; but can it all amount to a just indemnity for their labour? The treatment of servants in most countries, I grant, is very unjust; and in England, that boasted land of freedom, it is often extremely tyrannical. I have frequently, with indignation, heard gentlemen declare that they would never allow a servant to answer them; and ladies of the most exquisite sensibility, who were continually exclaiming against the cruelty of the vulgar to the brute creation, have in my presence forgot that their attendants had human feelings, as well as forms. I do not know a more agreeable sight than to see servants part of a family. By taking an interest, generally speaking, in their concerns, you inspire them with one for yours.

We must love our servants, or we shall never be sufficiently attentive to their happiness; and how can those
masters be attentive to their happiness, who living
above their fortunes, are more anxious to outshine their
neighbours than to allow their household the innocent
enjoyments they earn.

It is, in fact, much more difficult for servants who are
tantalized by seeing and preparing the dainties of which
they are not to partake, to remain honest, than the poor,
whose thoughts are not led from their homely fare; so
that, though the servants here are commonly thieves,
you seldom hear of house-breaking, or robbery on the
highway. The country is, perhaps, too thinly inhabited
to produce many of that description of thieves termed
footpads, or highwaymen. They are usually the spawn
of great cities; the effect of the spurious desires gener-
ated by wealth, rather than the desperate struggles of
poverty to escape from misery.

The enjoyment of the peasantry was drinking
brandy and coffee, before the latter was prohibited, and
the former not allowed to be privately distilled. The
wars carried on by the late king rendering it necessary
to increase the revenue, and retain the specie in the
country by every possible means.[1]

The taxes before the reign of Charles the twelfth
were inconsiderable.[2] Since then, the burden has contin-

---

1. Gustavus III needed money because he had waged a long and expensive war on Russia. The distilling of spirits was still controlled by the monarchy and, because of the tax revenue to be gained, citizens were encouraged
to drink freely; it is even reported that vats of liquor were located outside
the churches.

2. Charles XII ruled Sweden from 1697 to 1718 and was known as "the
Lion of the North" for all his war activities, which were expensive and
required taxation.

ually been growing heavier, and the price of provisions has proportionably increased; nay, the advantage accruing from the exportation of corn to France, and rye to Germany, will probably produce a scarcity in both Sweden and Norway, should not a peace put a stop to it this autumn;[3] for speculations of various kinds have already almost doubled the price.

Such are the effects of war, that it saps the vitals even of the neutral countries, who, obtaining a sudden influx of wealth, appear to be rendered flourishing by the destruction which ravages the hapless nations who are sacrificed to the ambition of their governors. I shall not, however, dwell on the vices, though they be of the most contemptible and embruting cast, to which a sudden accession of fortune gives birth, because I believe it may be delivered as an axiom that it is only in proportion to the industry necessary to acquire wealth, that a nation is really benefited by it.

The prohibition of drinking coffee, under a penalty, and the encouragement given to public distilleries, tend to impoverish the poor, who are not affected by the sumptuary laws; for the regent has lately laid very severe restraints on the article of dress, which the middling class of people found grievous because it obliged them to throw aside finery that might have lasted them for their lives.[4]

---

3. A peace in France, that is; in 1796, France was ruled by the Directory and was troubled internally as well as being at war with several other countries.
4. The ladies are only allowed to wear black and white silks, and plain muslins, besides other restrictions of a like nature. [Author's note.]

These may be termed vexations; still the death of the king, by saving them from the consequences his ambition would naturally have entailed on them, may be reckoned a blessing.

Besides, the French revolution has not only rendered all the crowned heads more cautious, but has so decreased every where (excepting amongst themselves) a respect for nobility, that the peasantry have not only lost their blind reverence for their seigniors, but complain, in a manly style, of oppressions which before they did not think of denominating such, because they were taught to consider themselves as a different order of beings. And, perhaps, the efforts which the aristocrats are making here, as well as in every other part of Europe, to secure their sway, will be the most effectual mode of undermining it; taking into the calculation, that the king of Sweden, like most of the potentates of Europe, has continually been augmenting his power by encroaching on the privileges of the nobles.

The well-bred Swedes of the capital are formed on the ancient French model; and they in general speak that language; for they have a knack at acquiring languages, with tolerable fluency. This may be reckoned an advantage in some respects; but it prevents the cultivation of their own, and any considerable advance in literary pursuits.

A sensible writer[5] has lately observed (I have not his work by me, therefore cannot quote his exact words), "that the Americans very wisely let the Europeans

---

5. See Mr. Cooper's *Account of America* [Author's note.] (See following note.)

make their books and fashions for them."[6] But I cannot coincide with him in this opinion. The reflection necessary to produce a certain number even of tolerable productions, augments, more than he is aware of, the mass of knowledge in the community. Desultory reading is commonly merely a pastime. But we must have an object to refer our reflections to, or they will seldom go below the surface. As in traveling, the keeping of a journal excites to many useful enquiries that would not have been thought of, had the traveller only determined to see all he could see, without ever asking himself for what purpose. Besides, the very dabbling in literature furnishes harmless topics of conversation; for the not having such subjects at hand, though they are often insupportably fatiguing, renders the inhabitants of little towns prying and censorious. Idleness, rather than ill-nature, gives birth to scandal, and to the observation of little incidents which narrows the mind. It is frequently only the fear of being talked of, which produces that puerile scrupulosity about trifles incompatible with an enlarged plan of usefulness, and with the basis of all moral principles—respect for the virtues which are not merely the virtues of convention.

I am, my friend, more and more convinced that a metropolis, or an abode absolutely solitary, is the best calculated for the improvement of the heart, as well as

---

6. Thomas Cooper, *Some Information Respecting America* (Dublin, 1794; rpt. in the Economic Classics, New York: Augustus M. Kelley, 1969, p. 64: "Literature in America is an amusement only—collateral to the occupation of the person who attends, (and but occasionally attends) to it. In Europe, it is a trade—a means of livelihood. The making of books is there as much a business as the selling of books. No wonder therefore it is better done in Europe than in America; or that with their usual good sense the Americans should permit you to be their manufacturers of literature, as well as of crockery or calicoes."

the understanding; whether we desire to become acquainted with man, nature, or ourselves. Mixing with mankind, we are obliged to examine our prejudices, and often imperceptibly lose, as we analyze them. And in the country, growing intimate with nature, a thousand little circumstances, unseen by vulgar eyes, give birth to sentiments dear to the imagination, and inquiries which expand the soul, particularly when cultivation has not smoothed into insipidity all its originality of character.

I love the country; yet whenever I see a picturesque situation chosen on which to erect a dwelling, I am always afraid of the improvements. It requires uncommon taste to form a whole, and to introduce accommodations and ornaments analogous with the surrounding scene.[7]

I visited, near Gothenburg, a house with improved

---

7. With respect to gardening in England, I think we often make an egregious blunder by introducing too much shade; not considering that the shade which our climate requires need not be very thick. If it keep off the intense heat of the sun, and afford a solitary retirement, it is sufficient. But in many great gardens, or pleasure-grounds, the sun's rays can scarcely ever penetrate. These may amuse the eye; yet they are not *home walks* to which the owner can retire to enjoy air and solitude; for, excepting during an extraordinary dry summer, they are damp and chill. For the same reason, grottoes are absurd in this temperate climate. An umbrageous tree will afford sufficient shelter from the most ardent heat, that we ever feel. To speak explicitly, the usefulness of a garden ought to be conspicuous, because it ought not to be planted for the season when nature wantons in her prime; for the whole country is then a garden—far sweeter. If not very extensive, I think a garden should contain more shrubs and flowers than lofty trees; and in order to admit the sun-beams to enliven our spring, autumn and winter, serpentine walks, the rage for the line of beauty, should be made to submit to convenience. Yet, in this country, a broad straight gravel walk is a great convenience for those who wish to take exercise in all seasons, after rain particularly. When the weather is fine, the meadows offer winding paths, far superior to the formal turnings that interrupt reflection, without amusing the fancy. [Author's note.]

land about it, with which I was particularly delighted. It was close to a lake embosomed in pine clad rocks. In one part of the meadows, your eye was directed to the broad expanse; in another, you were led into a shade, to see a part of it, in the form of a river, rush amongst the fragments of rocks and roots of trees; nothing seemed forced. One recess, particularly grand and solemn, amongst the towering cliffs, had a rude stone table, and seat, placed in it, that might have served for a druid's haunt; whilst a placid stream below enlivened the flowers on its margin, where light-footed elves would gladly have danced their airy rounds.

Here the hand of taste was conspicuous, though not obtrusive, and formed a contrast with another abode in the same neighbourhood, on which much money had been lavished: where Italian colonades were placed to excite the wonder of the rude craggs; and a stone staircase, to threaten with destruction a wooden house. Venuses and Apollos condemned to lie hid in snow three parts of the year, seemed equally displaced, and called the attention off from the surrounding sublimity, without inspiring any voluptuous sensations. Yet even these abortions of vanity have been useful. Numberless workmen have been employed, and the superintending artist has improved the labourers whose unskilfulness tormented him, by obliging them to submit to the discipline of rules. Adieu!

Your's affectionately.

LETTER IV

THE SEVERITY of the long Swedish winter tends to render the people sluggish; for, though this season has its peculiar pleasures, too much time is employed to guard against its inclemency. Still, as warm cloathing is absolutely necessary, the women spin, and the men weave, and by these exertions get a fence[1] to keep out the cold. I have rarely passed a knot of cottages without seeing cloth laid out to bleach; and when I entered, always found the women spinning or knitting.

A mistaken tenderness, however, for their children, makes them, even in summer, load them with flannels; and, having a sort of natural antipathy to cold water, the squalid appearance of the poor babes, not to speak of the noxious smell which flannel and rugs retain, seems a reply to a question I had often asked—Why I did not see more children in the villages I passed through? Indeed the children appear to be nipt in the bud, having neither the graces nor charms of their age. And this, I am persuaded, is much more owing to the ignorance of the mothers than to the rudeness of the climate. Rendered feeble by the continual perspiration

---

1. A defense or protection.

they are kept in, whilst every pore is absorbing unwholesome moisture, they give them, even at the breast,
brandy, salt fish, and every other crude substance,
which air and exercise enables the parent to digest.

The women of fortune here, as well as every where
else, have nurses to suckle their children; and the total
want of chastity in the lower class of women frequently
renders them very unfit for the trust.[2]

You have sometimes remarked to me the difference
of the manners of the country girls in England and in
America; attributing the reserve of the former to the
climate—to the absence of genial suns. But it must be
their stars, not the zephyrs gently stealing on their
senses, which here lead frail women astray.[3] —Who can
look at these rocks, and allow the voluptuousness of
nature to be an excuse for gratifying the desires it inspires? We must, therefore, find some other cause beside
voluptuousness, I believe, to account for the conduct of
the Swedish and American country girls; for I am led
to conclude, from all the observations I have made, that
there is always a mixture of sentiment and imagination
in voluptuousness, to which neither of them have much
pretension.

The country girls of Ireland and Wales equally feel
the first impulse of nature, which, restrained in England
by fear or delicacy, proves that society is there in a
more advanced state. Besides, as the mind is cultivated,

---

2. A reference to the possibility of syphilis in such women. See Introduction, p. xiv, for a brief discussion of Wollstonecraft's views on breast-feeding.

3. A free rendering of the couplet ("If weak women go astray/ The stars
are more at fault than they") which Wollstonecraft had used in *Thoughts on
the Education of Daughters* (1787), in a review in *The Analytical Review* (July,
1790, p. 302), and in *A Vindication of the Rights of Woman* (1792). I have been
unable to locate the source of the quotation.

and taste gains ground, the passions become stronger, and rest on something more stable than the casual sympathies of the moment. Health and idleness will always account for promiscuous amours; and in some degree I term every person idle, the exercise of whose mind does not bear some proportion to that of the body.

The Swedish ladies exercise neither sufficiently; of course, grow very fat at an early age; and when they have not this downy appearance, a comfortable idea, you will say, in a cold climate, they are not remarkable for fine forms. They have, however, mostly fine complexions; but indolence makes the lily soon displace the rose. The quantity of coffee, spices, and other things of that kind, with want of care, almost universally spoil their teeth, which contrast but ill with their ruby lips.

The manners of Stockholm are refined, I hear, by the introduction of gallantry; but in the country, romping and coarse freedoms, with coarser allusions, keep the spirits awake. In the article of cleanliness, the women, of all descriptions, seem very deficient; and their dress shews that vanity is more inherent in women than taste.

The men appear to have paid still less court to the graces. They are a robust, healthy race, distinguished for their common sense and turn for humour, rather than for wit or sentiment. I include not, as you may suppose, in this general character, some of the nobility and officers, who having travelled, are polite and well informed.

I must own to you, that the lower class of people here amuse and interest me much more than the middling, with their apish good breeding and prejudices. The sympathy and frankness of heart conspicuous in the peasantry produces even a simple gracefulness of deportment, which has frequently struck me as very picturesque; I have often also been touched by their extreme desire to oblige me, when I could not explain my wants, and by their earnest manner of expressing that desire. There is such a charm in tenderness! —It is so delightful to love our fellow-creatures, and meet the honest affections as they break forth. Still, my good friend, I begin to think that I should not like to live continually in the country, with people whose minds have such a narrow range. My heart would frequently be interested; but my mind would languish for more companionable society.

The beauties of nature appear to me now even more alluring than in my youth, because my intercourse with the world has formed, without vitiating my taste. But, with respect to the inhabitants of the country, my fancy has probably, when disgusted with artificial manners, solaced itself by joining the advantages of cultivation with the interesting sincerity of innocence, forgetting the lassitude that ignorance will naturally produce. I like to see animals sporting, and sympathize in their pains and pleasures. Still I love sometimes to view the human face divine,[4] and trace the soul, as well as the heart, in its varying lineaments.

A journey to the country, which I must shortly make, will enable me to extend my remarks. —Adieu!

---

4. Wollstonecraft may be remembering a phrase from William Blake, with whose works she was no doubt acquainted; in *Songs of Innocence,* line 11 of the poem "The Divine Image" reads, "And Love, the human form divine."

LETTER V

HAD I determined to travel in Sweden merely for pleasure, I should probably have chosen the road to Stockholm, though convinced, by repeated observation, that the manners of a people are best discriminated in the country. The inhabitants of the capital are all of the same genus; for the varieties in the species we must, therefore, search where the habitations of men are so separated as to allow the difference of climate to have its natural effect. And with this difference we are, perhaps, most forcibly struck at the first view, just as we form an estimate of the leading traits of a character at the first glance, of which intimacy afterwards makes us almost lose sight.

As my affairs called me to Stromstad (the frontier town of Sweden) in my way to Norway, I was to pass over, I heard, the most uncultivated part of the country. Still I believe that the grand features of Sweden are the same every where, and it is only the grand features that admit of description. There is an individuality in every prospect, which remains in the memory as forcibly depicted as the particular features that have arrested our attention; yet we cannot find words to discriminate that individuality so as to enable a stranger to say, this is the face, that the view. We may amuse by setting the imagination to work; but we cannot store the memory with a fact.

As I wish to give you a general idea of this country, I shall continue in my desultory manner to make such observations and reflections as the circumstances draw forth, without losing time, by endeavouring to arrange them.

Travelling in Sweden is very cheap, and even commodious, if you make but the proper arrangements. Here, as in other parts of the continent, it is necessary to have your own carriage, and to have a servant who can speak the language, if you are unacquainted with it. Sometimes a servant who can drive would be found very useful, which was our case, for I travelled in company with two gentlemen, one of whom had a German servant who drove very well. This was all the party; for not intending to make a long stay, I left my little girl behind me.

As the roads are not much frequented, to avoid waiting three or four hours for horses, we sent, as is the constant custom, an *avant courier* the night before, to order them at every post, and we constantly found them ready. Our first set I jokingly termed *requisition* horses;[1] but afterwards we had almost always little spirited animals that went on at a round pace.

The roads, making allowance for the ups and downs, are uncommonly good and pleasant. The expence, in-

---

1. A reference to the large size of horses usually demanded for service; they might more probably be used in war or emergency than, as the author suggests, for the rather simple matter of pulling a carriage from one post stop to the next.

cluding the postillions and other incidental things, does not amount to more than a shilling the Swedish mile.[2]

The inns are tolerable; but not liking the rye bread, I found it necessary to furnish myself with some wheaten before I set out. The beds too were particularly disagreeable to me. It seemed to me that I was sinking into a grave when I entered them; for, immersed in down placed in a sort of box, I expected to be suffocated before morning. The sleeping between two down beds, they do so even in summer, must be very unwholesome during any season; and I cannot conceive how the people can bear it, especially as the summers are very warm. But warmth they seem not to feel; and, I should think, were afraid of the air, by always keeping their windows shut. In the winter, I am persuaded, I could not exist in rooms thus closed up, with stoves heated in their manner, for they only put wood into them twice a day; and, when the stove is thoroughly heated, they shut the flue, not admitting any air to renew its elasticity, even when the rooms are crowded with company. These stoves are made of earthenware, and often in a form that ornaments an apartment, which is never the case with the heavy iron ones I have seen elsewhere. Stoves may be economical; but I like a fire, a wood one, in preference; and I am convinced that the current of air which it attracts renders this the best mode of warming rooms.

We arrived early the second evening at a little village called Quistram, where we had determined to pass the night; having been informed that we should not afterwards find a tolerable inn until we reached Stromstad.

Advancing towards Quistram, as the sun was begin-

---

2. A Swedish mile is nearly six English miles. [Author's note.]

ning to decline, I was particularly impressed by the beauty of the situation. The road was on the declivity of a rocky mountain, slightly covered with a mossy herbage and vagrant firs. At the bottom, a river, straggling amongst the recesses of stone, was hastening forward to the ocean and its grey rocks, of which we had a prospect on the left, whilst on the right it stole peacefully forward into the meadows, losing itself in a thickly wooded rising ground. As we drew near, the loveliest banks of wild flowers variegated the prospect, and promised to exhale odours to add to the sweetness of the air, the purity of which you could almost see, alas! not smell, for the putrifying herrings, which they use as manure, after the oil has been extracted, spread over the patches of earth, claimed by cultivation, destroyed every other.

It was intolerable, and entered with us into the inn, which was in other respects a charming retreat.

Whilst supper was preparing I crossed the bridge, and strolled by the river, listening to its murmurs. Approaching the bank, the beauty of which had attracted my attention in the carriage, I recognized many of my old acquaintance growing with great luxuriancy.[3]

Seated on it, I could not avoid noting an obvious remark. Sweden appeared to me the country in the world most proper to form the botanist and natural historian:[4] every object seemed to remind me of the creation of things, of the first efforts of sportive nature. When a country arrives at a certain state of perfection, it looks as if it were made so; and curiosity is not excited. Besides, in social life too many objects occur for

3. I.e., the "heart's ease" or wild pansies mentioned in Letter I.
4. An oblique reference to Linnaeus (Carl von Linné [1707–78]), the originator of the modern system of botany and a native of Sweden.

any to be distinctly observed by the generality of mankind; yet a contemplative man, or poet, in the country, I do not mean the country adjacent to cities, feels and sees what would escape vulgar eyes, and draws suitable inferences. This train of reflections might have led me further, in every sense of the word; but I could not escape from the detestable evaporation of the herrings, which poisoned all my pleasure.

After making a tolerable supper, for it is not easy to get fresh provisions on the road, I retired, to be lulled to sleep by the murmuring of a stream, of which I with great difficulty obtained sufficient to perform my daily ablutions.

The last battle between the Danes and Swedes, which gave new life to their ancient enmity, was fought at this place 1788; only seventeen or eighteen were killed; for the great superiority of the Danes and Norwegians obliged the Swedes to submit; but sickness, and a scarcity of provisions, proved very fatal to their opponents, on their return.[5]

It would be very easy to search for the particulars of this engagement in the publications of the day; but as this manner of filling my pages does not come within my plan, I probably should not have remarked that the battle was fought here, were it not to relate an anecdote which I had from good authority.

I noticed, when I first mentioned this place to you, that we descended a steep before we came to the inn; an immense ridge of rocks stretching out on one side. The inn was sheltered under them; and about a hundred

---

5. The allied Danes and Norwegians did not conquer Sweden, as this paragraph seems to indicate; rather, after the invasion, pressure from England, France, and Prussia forced the three countries to sign a peace agreement.

yards from it was a bridge that crossed the river, whose murmurs I have celebrated; it was not fordable. The Swedish general received orders to stop at the bridge, and dispute the passage; a most advantageous post for an army so much inferior in force: but the influence of beauty is not confined to courts. The mistress of the inn was handsome: when I saw her there were still some remains of beauty; and, to preserve her house, the general gave up the only tenable station. He was afterwards broke for contempt of orders.

Approaching the frontiers, consequently the sea, nature resumed an aspect ruder and ruder, or rather seemed the bones of the world waiting to be clothed with every thing necessary to give life and beauty. Still it was sublime.

The clouds caught their hue of the rocks that menaced them. The sun appeared afraid to shine, the birds ceased to sing, and the flowers to bloom; but the eagle fixed his nest high amongst the rocks, and the vulture hovered over this abode of desolation. The farm houses, in which only poverty resided, were formed of logs scarcely keeping off the cold and drifting snow; out of them the inhabitants seldom peeped, and the sports or prattling of children was neither seen nor heard. The current of life seemed congealed at the source: all were not frozen; for it was summer, you remember; but every thing appeared so dull, that I waited to see ice, in order to reconcile me to the absence of gaiety.

The day before, my attention had frequently been attracted by the wild beauties of the country we passed through.

The rocks which tossed their fantastic heads so high were often covered with pines and firs, varied in the most picturesque manner. Little woods filled up the recesses, when forests did not darken the scene; and vallies and glens, cleared of the trees, displayed a dazzling verdure which contrasted with the gloom of the shading pines. The eye stole into many a covert where tranquillity seemed to have taken up her abode, and the number of little lakes that continually presented themselves added to the peaceful composure of the scenery. The little cultivation which appeared did not break the enchantment, nor did castles rear their turrets aloft to crush the cottages, and prove that man is more savage than the natives of the woods. I heard of the bears, but never saw them stalk forth, which I was sorry for; I wished to have seen one in its wild state. In the winter, I am told, they sometimes catch a stray cow, which is a heavy loss to the owner.

The farms are small. Indeed most of the houses we saw on the road indicated poverty, or rather that the people could just live. Towards the frontiers they grew worse and worse in their appearance, as if not willing to put sterility itself out of countenance. No gardens smiled round the habitations, not a potatoe or cabbage to eat with the fish drying on a stick near the door. A little grain here and there appeared, the long stalks of which you might almost reckon. The day was gloomy when we passed over this rejected spot, the wind bleak, and winter seemed to be contending with nature, faintly struggling to change the season. Surely, thought I, if the sun ever shines here, it cannot warm these stones; moss only cleaves to them, partaking of their hardness; and nothing like vegetable life appears to chear with hope the heart.

So far from thinking that the primitive inhabitants of the world lived in a southern climate, where Paradise spontaneously arose, I am led to infer, from various circumstances, that the first dwelling of man happened to be a spot like this which led him to adore a sun so seldom seen; for this worship, which probably preceded that of demons or demi-gods, certainly never began in a southern climate, where the continual presence of the sun prevented its being considered as a good; or rather the want of it never being felt, this glorious luminary would carelessly have diffused its blessings without being hailed as a benefactor. Man must therefore have been placed in the north, to tempt him to run after the sun, in order that the different parts of the earth might be peopled. Nor do I wonder that hordes of barbarians always poured out of these regions to seek for milder climes, when nothing like cultivation attached them to the soil; especially when we take into the view that the adventuring spirit, common to man, is naturally stronger and more general during the infancy of society. The conduct of the followers of Mahomet, and the crusaders, will sufficiently corroborate my assertion.[6]

Approaching nearer to Stromstad, the appearance of the town proved to be quite in character with the country we had just passed through. I hesitated to use the word country, yet could not find another; still it would sound absurd to talk of fields of rocks.

---

6. Wollstonecraft is speculating on the origin of civilization, basing a culture's antiquity on the appearance of sun worship, which, she says, preceded the anthropomorphic worship of gods. She may be borrowing from Leibnitz's idea of the "pre-established harmony" of the universe to suggest that humans were intentionally placed in cold climates so that they would be inspired to "chase the sun" and thereby people the world. The last sentence is hard to understand for, while the Crusaders came from Northern Europe, a colder climate, to fight the Holy Wars, the origin and expansion of Islam was confined to the sunny, even torrid climates.

The town was built on, and under them. Three or four weather-beaten trees were shrinking from the wind; and the grass grew so sparingly, that I could not avoid thinking Dr. Johnson's hyperbolical assertion "that the the man merited well of his country who made a few blades of grass grow where they never grew before,"[7] might here have been uttered with strict propriety. The steeple likewise towered aloft; for what is a church, even amongst the Lutherans, without a steeple? But to prevent mischief in such an exposed situation, it is wisely placed on a rock at some distance, not to endanger the roof of the church.

Rambling about, I saw the door open, and entered, when to my great surprise I found the clergyman reading prayers, with only the clerk attending. I instantly thought of Swift's "Dearly beloved Roger";[8] but on enquiry I learnt that some one had died that morning, and in Sweden it is customary to pray for the dead.

The sun, who I suspected never dared to shine, began now to convince me that he came forth only to torment; for though the wind was still cutting, the rocks became intolerably warm under my feet; whilst the

---

7. While I do not find this exact phrase in any of Samuel Johnson's works, it is a rough expression of his often reiterated criticism of the barrenness of Scotland, for things which grow wild elsewhere must be cultivated there, and to plant a tree was nearly an act of patriotism. Johnson had mentioned the absence of vegetation with dismay in *Journey to the Western Islands of Scotland* (1775), and his attitude is well-chronicled in James Boswell's *Life of Johnson* (1791) and *Journal of a Tour to the Hebrides* (1785).

8. Lord Orrery, in his *Remarks* (1751), one of the earliest biographies of Jonathan Swift, tells that when Swift was in charge of a small church in Laracor, near Dublin, he faced, the first day, a church empty save for the presence of his faithful clerk Roger, whom he addressed, saying, "Dearly beloved Roger, the Scripture moveth you and me" (cited in Henry Craik, *The Life of Jonathan Swift* [London, 1894], 1:119).

herring effluvia, which I before found so very offensive, once more assailed me. I hastened back to the house of a merchant, the little sovereign of the place, because he was by far the richest, though not the mayor.

Here we were most hospitably received, and introduced to a very fine and numerous family. I have before mentioned to you the lillies of the north, I might have added, water lillies, for the complexion of many, even of the young women seem to be bleached on the bosom of snow. But in this youthful circle the roses bloomed with all their wonted freshness, and I wondered from whence the fire was stolen which sparkled in their fine blue eyes.

Here we slept; and I rose early in the morning to prepare for my little voyage to Norway. I had determined to go by water, and was to leave my companions behind; but not getting a boat immediately, and the wind being high and unfavourable, I was told that it was not safe to go to sea during such boisterous weather; I was therefore obliged to wait for the morrow, and had the present day on my hands; which I feared would be irksome, because the family, who possessed about a dozen French words amongst them, and not an English phrase, were anxious to amuse me, and would not let me remain alone in my room. The town we had already walked round and round; and if we advanced farther on the coast, it was still to view the same unvaried immensity of water, surrounded by barrenness.

The gentlemen wishing to peep into Norway, proposed going to Fredericshall, the first town, the distance was only three Swedish miles. There, and back again, was but a day's journey, and would not, I thought, interfere with my voyage. I agreed, and invited the eldest and prettiest of the girls to accompany us. I invited her, because I liked to see a beautiful face animated by pleasure, and to have an opportunity of regarding the country, whilst the gentlemen were amusing themselves with her.

I did not know, for I had not thought of it, that we were to scale some of the most mountainous cliffs of Sweden, in our way to the ferry which separates the two countries.

Entering amongst the cliffs, we were sheltered from the wind; warm sun-beams began to play, streams to flow, and groves of pines diversified the rocks. Sometimes they became suddenly bare and sublime. Once, in particular, after mounting the most terrific precipice, we had to pass through a tremendous defile, where the closing chasm seemed to threaten us with instant destruction, when turning quickly, verdant meadows and a beautiful lake relieved and charmed my eyes.

I have never travelled through Switzerland; but one of my companions assured me, that I should not there find any thing superior, if equal to the wild grandeur of these views.

As we had not taken this excursion into our plan, the horses had not been previously ordered, which obliged us to wait two hours at the first post. The day was wearing away. The road was so bad, that walking up the precipices consumed the time insensibly. But as we desired horses at each post ready at a certain hour, we reckoned on returning more speedily.

We stopt to dine at a tolerable farm. They brought us out ham, butter, cheese, and milk; and the charge was so moderate, that I scattered a little money amongst the children who were peeping at us, in order to pay them for their trouble.

Arrived at the ferry, we were still detained; for the people who attend at the ferries have a stupid kind of sluggishness in their manner, which is very provoking when you are in haste. At present I did not feel it; for scrambling up the cliffs, my eye followed the river as it rolled between the grand rocky banks; and to complete the scenery, they were covered with firs and pines, through which the wind rustled, as if it were lulling itself to sleep with the declining sun.

Behold us now in Norway; and I could not avoid feeling surprise at observing the difference in the manners of the inhabitants of the two sides of the river; for every thing shews that the Norwegians are more industrious and more opulent. The Swedes, for neighbours are seldom the best friends, accuse the Norwegians of knavery, and they retaliate by bringing a charge of hypocrisy against the Swedes. Local circumstances probably render both unjust, speaking from their feelings, rather than reason: and is this astonishing when we consider that most writers of travels have done the same, whose works have served as materials for the compilers of universal histories. All are eager to give a national character; which is rarely just, because they do not discriminate the natural from the acquired difference. The natural, I believe, on due consideration, will be found to consist merely in the degree of vivacity or thoughtfulness, pleasure, or pain, inspired by the climate, whilst the varieties which the forms of government, including religion, produce, are much more numerous and unstable.

A people have been characterized as stupid by nature; what a paradox! because they did not consider that slaves, having no object to stimulate industry, have not their faculties sharpened by the only thing that can exercise them, self-interest. Others have been brought forward as brutes, having no aptitude for the arts and scences, only because the progress of improvement had not reached that stage which produces them.

Those writers who have considered the history of man, or of the human mind, on a more enlarged scale, have fallen into similar errors, not reflecting that the passions are weak where the necessaries of life are too hardly or too easily obtained.

Travellers who require that every nation should resemble their native country, had better stay at home. It is, for example, absurd to blame a people for not having that degree of personal cleanliness and elegance of manners which only refinement of taste produces, and will produce every where in proportion as society attains a general polish. The most essential service, I presume, that authors could render to society, would be to promote inquiry and discussion, instead of making those dogmatical assertions which only appear calculated to gird the human mind round with imaginary circles, like the paper globe which represents the one he inhabits.

This spirit of inquiry is the characteristic of the present century, from which the succeeding will, I am persuaded, receive a great accumulation of knowledge; and doubtless its diffusion will in a great measure destroy the factitious national characters which have been supposed permanent, though only rendered so by the permanency of ignorance.

Arriving at Fredericshall, at the siege of which Charles XII lost his life,[9] we had only time to take a

---

9. An absolute monarch and an ambitious military man, as well as a model soldier who shared accommodations and food with his men, Charles XII of Sweden had assembled one of the most effective armies in history. He was killed by a bullet at close range as he watched the siege of Fredrikshald in 1718. Even though a modern disinterment has suggested otherwise, reputable historians still suggest that Charles was murdered by an assassin.

transient view of it, wilst they were preparing us some refreshment.

Poor Charles! I thought of him with respect. I have always felt the same for Alexander; with whom he has been classed as a madman, by several writers, who have reasoned superficially, confounding the morals of the day with the few grand principles on which unchangeable morality rests. Making no allowance for the ignorance and prejudices of the period, they do not perceive how much they themselves are indebted to general improvement for the acquirements, and even the virtues, which they would not have had the force of mind to attain, by their individual exertions in a less advanced state of society.

The evening was fine, as is usual at this season; and the refreshing odour of the pine woods became more perceptible; for it was nine o'clock when we left Fredericshall. At the ferry we were detained by a dispute relative to our Swedish passport, which we did not think of getting countersigned in Norway. Midnight was coming on; yet it might with such propriety have been termed the noon of night, that had Young ever travelled towards the north, I should not have wondered at his becoming enamoured of the moon.[10] But it is not the queen of night alone who reigns here in all her splendor, though the sun, loitering just below the horizon, decks her with a golden tinge from his car, illuminating the cliffs that hide him; the heavens also, of a clear softened blue, throw her forward, and the evening star appears a lesser moon to the naked eye. The

10. Edward Young's long poem *Night Thoughts* (published 1742–45) consists of nine books, or "nights"; in Book III he invokes the moon, "Day's soft-eyed sister," to inspire him.

huge shadows of the rocks, fringed with firs, concentrating the views, without darkening them, excited that tender melancholy which, sublimating the imagination, exalts, rather than depresses the mind.

My companions fell asleep:—fortunately they did not snore; and I contemplated, fearless of idle questions, a night such as I had never before seen or felt to charm the senses, and calm the heart. The very air was balmy, as it freshened into morn, producing the most voluptuous sensations. A vague pleasurable sentiment absorbed me, as I opened my bosom to the embraces of nature; and my soul rose to its author, with the chirping of the solitary birds, which began to feel, rather than see, advancing day. I had leisure to mark its progress. The grey morn, streaked with silvery rays, ushered in the orient beams,—how beautifully varying into purple!— yet, I was sorry to lose the soft watry clouds which preceded them, exciting a kind of expectation that made me almost afraid to breathe, lest I should break the charm. I saw the sun—and sighed.

One of my companions, now awake, perceiving that the postillion had mistaken the road, began to swear at him, and roused the other two, who reluctantly shook off sleep.

We had immediately to measure back our steps, and did not reach Stromstad before five in the morning.

The wind had changed in the night, and my boat was ready.

A dish of coffee, and fresh linen, recruited my spirits; and I directly set out again for Norway; purposing to land much higher up the coast.

Wrapping my great coat round me, I lay down on some sails at the bottom of the boat, its motion rocking me to rest, till a discourteous wave interrupted my slumbers, and obliged me to rise and feel a solitariness which was not so soothing as that of the past night.

Adieu!

LETTER VI

THE SEA was boisterous; but, as I had an experienced pilot, I did not apprehend any danger. Sometimes I was told, boats are driven far out and lost. However, I seldom calculate chances so nicely—sufficient for the day is the obvious evil![1]

We had to steer amongst islands and huge rocks, rarely losing sight of the shore, though it now and then appeared only a mist that bordered the water's edge. The pilot assured me that the numerous harbours on the Norway coast were very safe, and the pilot-boats were always on the watch. The Swedish side is very dangerous, I am also informed; and the help of experience is not often at hand, to enable strange vessels to steer clear of the rocks, which lurk below the water, close to the shore.

There are no tides here, nor in the cattegate;[2] and, what appeared to me a consequence, no sandy beach. Perhaps this observation has been made before; but it did not occur to me till I saw the waves continually

---

1. Matthew 6:34: "Sufficient unto the day is the evil thereof."
2. The Kattegat is the inlet between Sweden and Denmark.

beating against the bare rocks, without ever receding to leave a sediment to harden.

The wind was fair, till we had to tack about in order to enter Laurvig, where we arrived towards three o'clock in the afternoon. It is a clean, pleasant town, with a considerable iron-work, which gives life to it.

As the Norwegians do not frequently see travellers, they are very curious to know their business, and who they are—so curious that I was half tempted to adopt Dr. Franklin's plan, when travelling in America, where they are equally prying, which was to write on a paper, for public inspection, my name, from whence I came, where I was going, and what was my business.[3] But if I were importuned by their curiosity, their friendly gestures gratified me. A woman, coming alone, interested them. And I know not whether my weariness gave me a look of peculiar delicacy; but they approached to assist me, and enquire after my wants, as if they were afraid to hurt, and wished to protect me. The sympathy I inspired, thus dropping down from the clouds in a strange land, affected me more than it would have done, had not my spirits been harassed by various causes—by much thinking—musing almost to madness —and even by a sort of weak melancholy that hung about my heart at parting with my daughter for the first time.

---

3. Franklin never directly mentions wearing a sign to identify himself to his curious countrymen, but he does discuss the "prying" Americans who when Indians come into colonists' villages are most uncivil: "when any of them come into our Towns, our people are apt to crowd round them, gaze upon them, and incommode them where they desire to be private." The "savages" of course are far more civilized and never "enter a Village abruptly without giving Notice of their Approach" ("The Savages of North America" in *Works*, ed. Albert Henry Smythe [New York, 1905–07], 10:101–2.)

You know that as a female I am particularly attached to her—I feel more than a mother's fondness and anxiety, when I reflect on the dependent and oppressed state of her sex. I dread lest she should be forced to sacrifice her heart to her principles, or principles to her heart. With trembling hand I shall cultivate sensibility, and cherish delicacy of sentiment, lest, whilst I lend fresh blushes to the rose, I sharpen the thorns that will wound the breast I would fain guard—I dread to unfold her mind, lest it should render her unfit for the world she is to inhabit—Hapless woman! what a fate is thine!

But whither am I wandering? I only meant to tell you that the impression the kindness of the simple people made visible on my countenance increased my sensibility to a painful degree. I wished to have had a room to myself; for their attention, and rather distressing observation, embarrassed me extremely. Yet, as they would bring me eggs, and make my coffee, I found I could not leave them without hurting their feelings of hospitality.

It is customary here for the host and hostess to welcome their guests as master and mistress of the house.

My clothes, in their turn, attracted the attention of the females; and I could not help thinking of the foolish vanity which makes many women so proud of the observation of strangers as to take wonder very gratuitously for admiration. This error they are very apt to fall into; when arrived in a foreign country, the populace stare at them as they pass: yet the make of a cap, or the singularity of a gown, is often the cause of the flattering attention, which afterwards supports a fantastic superstructure of self-conceit.

Not having brought a carriage over with me, expecting to have met a person where I landed, who was

immediately to have procured me one, I was detained
whilst the good people of the inn sent round to all their
acquaintance to search for a vehicle. A rude sort of
cabriole[4] was at last found, and a driver half drunk, who
was not less eager to make a good bargain on that
account. I had a Danish captain of a ship and his mate
with me: the former was to ride on horseback, at which
he was not very expert, and the latter to partake of my
seat. The driver mounted behind to guide the horses,
and flourish the whip over our shoulders; he would not
suffer the reins out of his own hands. There was something
so grotesque in our appearance, that I could not
avoid shrinking into myself when I saw a gentleman-
like man in the group which crowded round the door
to observe us. I could have broken the driver's whip for
cracking to call the women and children together; but
seeing a significant smile on the face, I had before remarked, I burst into a laugh, to allow him to do so too,
—and away we flew. This is not a flourish of the pen;
for we actually went on full gallop a long time, the
horses being very good; indeed I have never met with
better, if so good, post-horses, as in Norway; they are
of a stouter make than the English horses, appear to be
well fed, and are not easily tired.

I had to pass over, I was informed, the most fertile
and best cultivated tract of country in Norway. The
distance was three Norwegian miles, which are longer
than the Swedish.[5] The roads were very good; the
farmers are obliged to repair them; and we scampered
through a great extent of country in a more improved

---

4. A *cabriolet* is a small two-wheeled carriage drawn by one horse.
5. See Wollstonecraft's Supplementary Notes, below, p. 199, for English
equivalents of Norwegian miles.

state than any I had viewed since I left England. Still there was sufficient of hills, dales, and rocks, to prevent the idea of a plain from entering the head, or even of such scenery as England and France afford. The prospects were also embellished by water, rivers, and lakes, before the sea proudly claimed my regard; and the road running frequently through lofty groves, rendered the landscapes beautiful, though they were not so romantic as those I had lately seen with such delight.

It was late when I reached Tonsberg; and I was glad to go to bed at a decent inn. The next morning, the 17th of July, conversing with the gentlemen with whom I had business to transact, I found that I should be detained at Tonsberg three weeks; and I lamented that I had not brought my child with me.

The inn was quiet, and my room so pleasant, commanding a view of the sea, confined by an amphitheatre of hanging woods, that I wished to remain there, though no one in the house could speak English or French. The mayor, my friend, however, sent a young woman to me who spoke a little English, and she agreed to call on me twice a day, to receive my orders, and translate them to my hostess.

My not understanding the language was an excellent pretext for dining alone, which I prevailed on them to let me do at a late hour; for the early dinners in Sweden had entirely deranged my day. I could not alter it there, without disturbing the economy of a family where I was as a visitor; necessity having forced me to accept of an invitation from a private family, the lodgings were so incommodious.

Amongst the Norwegians I had the arrangement of my own time; and I determined to regulate it in such a manner, that I might enjoy as much of their sweet summer as I possibly could;—short, it is true; but "passing sweet."[6]

I never endured a winter in this rude clime; consequently it was not the contrast, but the real beauty of the season which made the present summer appear to me the finest I had ever seen. Sheltered from the north and eastern winds, nothing can exceed the salubrity, the soft freshness of the western gales. In the evening they also die away; the aspen leaves tremble into stillness, and reposing nature seems to be warmed by the moon, which here assumes a genial aspect: and if a light shower has chanced to fall with the sun, the juniper the underwood of the forest, exhales a wild perfume, mixed with a thousand nameless sweets, that, soothing the heart, leave images in the memory which the imagination will ever hold dear.

Nature is the nurse of sentiment,—the true source of taste;—yet what misery, as well as rapture, is produced by a quick perception of the beautiful and sublime, when it is exercised in observing animated nature, when every beauteous feeling and emotion excites responsive sympathy, and the harmonized soul sinks into melancholy, or rises to extasy, just as the chords are touched, like the aeolian harp agitated by the changing wind. But how dangerous is it to foster these sentiments in such an imperfect state of existence; and how difficult to eradicate them when an affection for mankind, a passion for an individual, is but the unfolding of that love which embraces all that is great and beautiful.

When a warm heart has received strong impressions, they are not to be effaced. Emotions become sentiments;

---

6. William Cowper, *Retirement,* line 737: "How sweet, how passing sweet, is solitude!"

and the imagination renders even transient sensations permanent, by fondly retracing them. I cannot, without a thrill of delight, recollect views I have seen, which are not to be forgotten,—nor looks I have felt in every nerve which I shall never more meet. The grave has closed over a dear friend, the friend of my youth;[7] still she is present with me, and I hear her soft voice warbling as I stray over the heath. Fate has separated me from another, the fire of whose eyes, tempered by infantine tenderness, still warms my breast; even when gazing on these tremendous cliffs, sublime emotions absorb my soul. And, smile not, if I add, that the rosy tint of morning reminds me of a suffusion, which will never more charm my senses, unless it reappears on the cheeks of my child. Her sweet blushes I may yet hide in my bosom, and she is still too young to ask why starts the tear, so near akin to pleasure and pain?

I cannot write any more at present. Tomorrow we will talk of Tonsberg.

---

7. Wollstonecraft's friend and soul-mate, Fanny Blood, had travelled to Portugal in February 1785 to marry Hugh Skeys and died in Mary's arms after childbirth that November.

LETTER VII

THOUGH the king of Denmark be an absolute monarch, yet the Norwegians appear to enjoy all the blessings of freedom.[1] Norway may be termed a sister
kingdom; but the people have no viceroy to lord it over
them, and fatten his dependants with the fruit of their
labour.

There are only two counts in the whole country,
who have estates, and exact some feudal observances
from their tenantry. All the rest of the country is divided into small farms, which belong to the cultivator.
It is true, some few, appertaining to the church, are let;
but always on a lease for life, generally renewed in
favour of the eldest son, who has this advantage, as well
as a right to a double portion of the property. But the
value of the farm is estimated; and after his portion is
assigned to him, he must be answerable for the residue
to the remaining part of the family.

Every farmer, for ten years, is obliged to attend annually about twelve days, to learn the military exercise;

---

1. Norway had been part of Denmark since the union of 1389; it was
then ruled by Sweden from 1815 to 1905, when it emerged as an independent state.

but it is always at a small distance from his dwelling, and does not lead him into any new habits of life.

There are about six thousand regulars also, garrisoned at Christiania and Fredericshall, which are equally reserved, with the militia, for the defence of their own country. So that when the prince royal passed into Sweden, in 1788, he was obliged to request, not command, them to accompany him on this expedition.[2]

These corps are mostly composed of the sons of the cottagers, who being labourers on the farms, are allowed a few acres to cultivate for themselves. These men voluntarily enlist; but it is only for a limited period, (six years), at the expiration of which they have the liberty of retiring. The pay is only two-pence a day, and bread; still, considering the cheapness of the country, it is more than sixpence in England.

The distribution of landed property into small farms, produces a degree of equality which I have seldom seen elsewhere; and the rich being all merchants, who are obliged to divide their personal fortune amongst their children, the boys always receiving twice as much as the girls, property has not a chance of accumulating till overgrown wealth destroys the balance of liberty.

You will be surprised to hear me talk of liberty; yet the Norwegians appear to me to be the most free community I have ever observed.

The mayor of each town or district, and the judges in the country, exercise an authority almost patriarchal. They can do much good, but little harm, as every individual can appeal from their judgment: and as they may

2. The Crown Prince, the future Frederick VI, son of Christian VI and Caroline Matilda, passed through to the brief war with Sweden in 1788 (referred to in Letter V, note 5, above).

always be forced to give a reason for their conduct, it is generally regulated by prudence. "They have not time to learn to be tyrants," said a gentleman to me, with whom I discussed the subject.

The farmers not fearing to be turned out of their farms, should they displease a man in power, and having no vote to be commanded at an election for a mock representative, are a manly race; for not being obliged to submit to any debasing tenure, in order to live, or advance themselves in the world, they act with an independent spirit. I never yet have heard of any thing like domineering, or oppression, excepting such as has arisen from natural causes. The freedom the people enjoy may, perhaps, render them a little litigious, and subject them to the impositions of cunning practitioners of the law; but the authority of office is bounded, and the emoluments of it do not destroy its utility.

Last year a man, who had abused his power, was cashiered, on the representation of the people to the bailiff of the district.

There are four in Norway, who might with propriety be termed sheriffs; and, from their sentence, an appeal, by either party, may be made to Copenhagen.

Near most of the towns are commons, on which the cows of all the inhabitants, indiscriminately, are allowed to graze. The poor, to whom a cow is necessary, are almost supported by it. Besides, to render living more easy, they all go out to fish in their own boats; and fish is their principal food.

The lower class of people in the towns are in general sailors; and the industrious have usually little ventures of their own that serve to render the winter comfortable.

With respect to the country at large, the importation is considerably in favour of Norway.

They are forbidden, at present, to export corn or rye, on account of the advanced price.

The restriction which most resembles the painful subordination of Ireland,[3] is that vessels, trading to the West Indies, are obliged to pass by their own ports, and unload their cargoes at Copenhagen, which they afterwards re-ship. The duty is indeed inconsiderable; but the navigation being dangerous, they run a double risk.

There is an excise on all articles of consumption brought to the towns; but the officers are not strict; and it would be reckoned invidious to enter a house to search, as in England.

The Norwegians appear to me a sensible, shrewd people, with little scientific knowledge, and still less taste for literature: but they are arriving at the epoch which precedes the introduction of the arts and sciences.

Most of the towns are sea-ports, and sea-ports are not favourable to improvement. The captains acquire a little superficial knowledge by travelling, which their indefatigable attention to the making of money prevents their digesting; and the fortune that they thus laboriously acquire, is spent, as it usually is in towns of this description, in shew and good living. They love their country, but have not much public spirit.[4] Their exer-

---

3. Ireland was not permitted by England to export wool and linen; England itself took the goods and collected the tariff. As a result, of course, there was a thriving smuggling operation in eighteenth-century Ireland.

4. The grand virtues of the heart particularly the enlarged humanity which extends to the whole human race, depend more on the understanding, I believe, than is generally imagined. [Author's note.]

tions are, generally speaking, only for their families; which I conceive will always be the case, till politics, becoming a subject of discussion, enlarges the heart by opening the understanding. The French revolution will have this effect. They sing at present, with great glee, many republican songs, and seem earnestly to wish that the republic may stand; yet they appear very much attached to their prince royal; and, as far as rumour can give an idea of a character, he appears to merit their attachment. When I am at Copenhagen, I shall be able to ascertain on what foundation their good opinion is built; at present I am only the echo of it.

In the year 1788 he travelled through Norway; and acts of mercy gave dignity to the parade, and interest to the joy, his presence inspired. At this town he pardoned a girl condemned to die for murdering an illegitimate child, a crime seldom committed in this country. She is since married, and become the careful mother of a family. This might be given as an instance, that a desperate act is not always a proof of an incorrigible depravity of character; the only plausible excuse that has been brought forward to justify the infliction of capital punishments.

I will relate two or three other anecdotes to you; for the truth of which I will not vouch, because the facts were not of sufficient consequence for me to take much pains to ascertain them; and, true or false, they evince that the people like to make a kind of mistress of their prince.

An officer, mortally wounded at the ill-advised battle of Quistram, desired to speak with the prince; and, with his dying breath, earnestly recommended to his care a young woman of Christiania, to whom he was engaged. When the prince returned there, a ball was given by the chief inhabitants. He inquired whether this unfortunate girl was invited, and requested that she might, though of the second class. The girl came; she was pretty; and finding herself amongst her superiors, bashfully sat down as near the door as possible, nobody taking notice of her. Shortly after, the prince entering, immediately inquired for her, and asked her to dance, to the mortification of the rich dames. After it was over he handed her to the top of the room, and placing himself by her, spoke of the loss she had sustained, with tenderness, promising to provide for any one she should marry,— as the story goes. She is since married, and he has not forgotten his promise.

A little girl, during the same expedition, in Sweden, who informed him that the logs of a bridge were cut underneath, was taken by his orders to Christiania, and put to school at his expence.

Before I retail other beneficial effects of his journey, it is necessary to inform you that the laws here are mild, and do not punish capitally for any crime but murder, which seldom occurs. Every other offence merely subjects the delinquent to imprisonment and labour in the castle, or rather arsenal, at Christiania, and the fortress at Fredericshall. The first and second conviction produces a sentence for a limited number of years,—two, three, five, or seven, proportioned to the atrocity of the crime. After the third he is whipped, branded in the forehead, and condemned to perpetual slavery. This is the ordinary march of justice. For some flagrant breaches of trust, or acts of wanton cruelty, criminals have been condemned to slavery for life, the first time of conviction, but not frequently. The number of these slaves do not, I am informed, amount to more than an hundred, which is not considerable, compared with the population, upwards of eight hundred thousand. Should I pass through Christiania, on my return to Gothenburg, I shall probably have an opportunity of learning other particulars.

There is also a house of correction at Christiania for trifling misdemeanors, where the women are confined to labour and imprisonment even for life. The state of the prisoners was represented to the prince; in consequence of which, he visited the arsenal and house of correction. The slaves at the arsenal were loaded with irons of a great weight; he ordered them to be lightened as much as possible.

The people in the house of correction were commanded not to speak to him; but four women, condemned to remain there for life, got into the passage, and fell at his feet. He granted them a pardon; and inquiring respecting the treatment of the prisoners, he was informed that they were frequently whipt going in, and coming out; and for any fault, at the discretion of the inspectors. This custom he humanely abolished; though some of the principal inhabitants, whose situation in life had raised them above the temptation of stealing, were of opinion that these chastisements were necessary and wholesome.

In short, every thing seems to announce that the prince really cherishes the laudable ambition of fulfilling the duties of his station. This ambition is cherished and directed by the count Bernstorf, the prime minister of Denmark, who is universally celebrated for his abilities and virtue. The happiness of the people is a substantial eulogium; and, from all I can gather, the inhabitants of Denmark and Norway are the least oppressed people of Europe. The press is free. They translate any of the

French publications of the day, deliver their opinion on the subject, and discuss those it leads to with great freedom, and without fearing to displease the government.

On the subject of religion they are likewise becoming tolerant, at least, and perhaps have advanced a step further in free-thinking. One writer has ventured to deny the divinity of Jesus Christ, and to question the necessity or utility of the christian system, without being considered universally as a monster, which would have been the case a few years ago. They have translated many German works on education; and though they have not adopted any of their plans, it is become a subject of discussion. There are some grammar and free schools; but, from what I hear, not very good ones. All the children learn to read, write, and cast accounts, for the purposes of common life. They have no university; and nothing that deserves the name of science is taught; nor do individuals, by pursuing any branch of knowledge, excite a degree of curiosity which is the forerunner of improvement. Knowledge is not absolutely necessary to enable a considerable portion of the community to live; and, till it is, I fear, it never becomes general.

In this country, where minerals abound, there is not one collection: and, in all probability, I venture a conjecture, the want of mechanical and chemical knowledge renders the silver mines unproductive; for the quantity of silver obtained every year is not sufficient to defray the expenses. It has been urged, that the employment of such a number of hands is very beneficial. But a positive loss is never to be done away; and the men, thus employed, would naturally find some other means of living, instead of being thus a dead weight on government, or rather on the community from whom its revenue is drawn.

About three English miles from Tonsberg there is a salt work, belonging, like all their establishments, to government, in which they employ above an hundred and fifty men, and maintain nearly five hundred people, who earn their living. The clear profit, an increasing one, amounts to two thousand pounds sterling. And as the eldest son of the inspector, an ingenious young man, has been sent by the government to travel, and acquire some mathematical and chemical knowledge in Germany, it has a chance of being improved. He is the only person I have met with here, who appears to have a scientific turn of mind. I do not mean to assert that I have not met with others, who have a spirit of inquiry.

The salt-works at St. Ubes are basons in the sand, and the sun produces the evaporation; but here there is no beach. Besides, the heat of summer is so short-lived, that it would be idle to contrive machines for such an inconsiderable portion of the year. They therefore always use fires; and the whole establishment appears to be regulated with judgment.

The situation is well chosen and beautiful. I do not find, from the observation of a person who has resided here for forty years, that the sea advances or recedes on this coast.

I have already remarked, that little attention is paid to education, excepting reading, writing, and the rudiments of arithmetic; I ought to have added, that a catechism is carefully taught, and the children obliged to read in the churches, before the congregation, to prove that they are not neglected.

Degrees, to enable any one to practise any profession, must be taken at Copenhagen; and the people of this country, having the good sense to perceive that men who are to live in a community should at least acquire the elements of their knowledge, and form their youthful attachments there, are seriously endeavouring to establish an university in Norway. And Tonsberg, as a centrical place in the best part of the country, had the most suffrages; for, experiencing the bad effects of a metropolis, they have determined not to have it in or near Christiania. Should such an establishment take place, it will promote inquiry throughout the country, and give a new face to society. Premiums have been offered, and prize questions written, which I am told have merit. The building college-halls, and other appendages of the seat of science, might enable Tonsberg to recover its pristine consequence; for it is one of the most ancient towns of Norway, and once contained nine churches. At present there are only two. One is a very old structure, and has a gothic respectability about it, which scarcely amounts to grandeur, because, to render a gothic pile grand, it must have a huge unwieldiness of appearance. The chapel of Windsor may be an exception to this rule; I mean before it was in its present *nice, clean* state.[5] When I first saw it, the pillars within had acquired, by time, a sombre hue, which accorded with the architecture; and the gloom increased its dimensions to the eye by hiding its parts; but now it all bursts on the view at once; and the sublimity has van-

---

5. St. George's Chapel at Windsor Castle had undergone some restoration and refurbishing under George III; Wollstonecraft had visited Windsor during her employment from 1778 to 1780 as a companion to Mrs. Dawson of Bath.

ished before the brush and broom; for it has been white-
washed and scraped till it is become as bright and neat
as the pots and pans in a notable house-wife's kitchen—
yes; the very spurs on the recumbent knights were deprived of their venerable rust, to give a striking proof
that a love of order in trifles, and taste for proportion
and arrangement, are very distinct. The glare of light
thus introduced, entirely destroys the sentiment these
piles are calculated to inspire; so that, when I heard
something like a jig from the organ-loft, I thought it an
excellent hall for dancing or feasting. The measured
pace of thought with which I had entered the cathedral,
changed into a trip; and I bounded on the terrace, to see
the royal family, with a number of ridiculous images in
my head, that I shall not now recall.

The Norwegians are fond of music; and every little
church has an organ. In the church I have mentioned,
there is an inscription importing that a king,[6] James the
sixth, of Scotland, and first of England, who came with

---

6. "Anno 1589, St. Martin's Day, which was the 11th Day of November,
on a Tuesday, came the high-born Prince and Lord Jacob Stuart, King in
Scotland, to this Town, and the 25th Sunday after Trinity (Sunday:) which
was the 16th Day of November, stood his Grace in this Pew, and heard
Scotch Preaching from the 23d Psalm, 'The Lord is my Shepherd,' &c.
which M. David Lentz, Preacher in Lith, then preached between 10 and
12."
    The above is an inscription which stands in St. Mary's church, in Tons-
berg.
    It is known that king James the sixth went to Norway, to marry Princess
Anna, the daughter of Frederick the second, and sister to Christian the
fourth; and that the wedding was performed at Opslo (now Christiania),
where the princess, by contrary winds, was detained; but that the king,
during this voyage, was at Tonsberg, nobody would have known, if an
inscription, in remembrance of it, had not been placed in this church. [Au-
thor's note.]

more than princely gallantry, to escort his bride home, stood there, and heard divine service.

There is a little recess full of coffins, which contains bodies embalmed long since—so long, that there is not even a tradition to lead to a guess at their names.

A desire of preserving the body seems to have prevailed in most countries of the world, futile as it is to term it a preservation, when the noblest parts are immediately sacrificed merely to save the muscles, skin and bone from rottenness. When I was shewn these human petrifactions, I shrunk back with disgust and horror. "Ashes to ashes!" thought I—"Dust to dust!"—If this be not dissolution, it is something worse than natural decay. It is treason against humanity, thus to lift up the awful veil which would fain hide its weakness. The grandeur of the active principle is never more strongly felt than at such a sight; for nothing is so ugly as the human form when deprived of life, and thus dried into stone, merely to preserve the most disgusting image of death. The contemplation of noble ruins produces a melancholy that exalts the mind. —We take a retrospect of the exertions of man, the fate of empires and their rulers; and marking the grand destruction of ages, it seems the necessary change of time leading to improvement. —Our very soul expands, and we forget our littleness; how painfully brought to our recollection by such vain attempts to snatch from decay what is destined so soon to perish. Life, what art thou? Where goes this breath? this *I*, so much alive? In what element will it mix, giving or receiving fresh energy? —What will break the enchantment of animation? —For worlds, I would not see a form I loved—embalmed in my heart —thus sacrilegiously handled! —Pugh! my stomach turns. —Is this all the distinction of the rich in the grave? —They had better quietly allow the scythe of equality to mow them down with the common mass, than struggle to become a monument of the instability of human greatness.

The teeth, nails and skin were whole, without appearing black like the Egyptian mummies; and some silk, in which they had been wrapt, still preserved its colour, pink, with tolerable freshness.

I could not learn how long the bodies had been in this state, in which they bid fair to remain till the day of judgment, if there is to be such a day; and before that time, it will require some trouble to make them fit to appear in company with angels, without disgracing humanity. —God bless you! I feel a conviction that we have some perfectible principle in our present vestment, which will not be destroyed just as we begin to be sensible of improvement; and I care not what habit it next puts on, sure that it will be wisely formed to suit a higher state of existence. Thinking of death makes us tenderly cling to our affections—with more than usual tenderness, I therefore assure you that I am your's, wishing that the temporary death of absence may not endure longer than is absolutely necessary.

LETTER VIII

TONSBERG was formerly the residence of one of the little sovereigns of Norway; and on an adjacent mountain the vestiges of a fort remain, which was battered down by the Swedes; the entrance of the bay lying close to it.

Here I have frequently strayed, sovereign of the waste, I seldom met any human creature; and sometimes, reclining on the mossy down, under the shelter of a rock, the prattling of the sea amongst the pebbles has lulled me to sleep—no fear of any rude satyr's approaching to interrupt my repose. Balmy were the slumbers, and soft the gales, that refreshed me, when I awoke to follow, with an eye vaguely curious, the white sails, as they turned the cliffs, or seemed to take shelter under the pines which covered the little islands that so gracefully rose to render the terrific ocean beautiful. The fishermen were calmly casting their nets; whilst the seagulls hovered over the unruffled deep. Every thing seemed to harmonize into tranquillity— even the mournful call of the bittern was in cadence with the tinkling bells on the necks of the cows, that, pacing slowly one after the other, along an inviting path in the vale below, were repairing to the cottages to be milked. With what ineffable pleasure have I not gazed—and gazed again, losing my breath through my eyes—my very soul diffused itself in the scene—and, seeming to become all senses, glided in the scarcely-agitated waves, melted in the freshening breeze, or, taking its flight with fairy wing, to the misty mountains which bounded the prospect, fancy tript over new lawns, more beautiful even than the lovely slopes on the winding shore before me. —I pause, again breathless, to trace, with renewed delight, sentiments which entranced me, when, turning my humid eyes from the expanse below to the vault above, my sight pierced the fleecy clouds that softened the azure brightness; and, imperceptibly recalling the reveries of childhood, I bowed before the awful throne of my Creator, whilst I rested on its footstool.

You have sometimes wondered, my dear friend, at the extreme affection of my nature—But such is the temperature of my soul—It is not the vivacity of youth, the hey-day of existence. For years have I endeavoured to calm an impetuous tide—labouring to make my feelings take an orderly course. —It was striving against the stream. —I must love and admire with warmth, or I sink into sadness. Tokens of love which I have received have rapt me in elysium—purifying the heart they enchanted. —My bosom still glows. —Do not saucily ask, repeating Sterne's question, "Maria, is it still so warm?"[1] Sufficiently, O my God! has it been chilled by

---

1. The reference is to the words of Yorick, the traveller, to the sorrowful young woman Maria, in Laurence Sterne's *A Sentimental Journey*. Yorick is in tears at the story of Maria's misfortunes, and as he uses his handkerchief she notices that it is too drenched to be effective and says she will take it to the stream to wash it. When Yorick asks where she will dry it, she says, in her bosom, and Yorick asks tenderly, "And is your heart still so warm, Maria?" (Sterne, *A Sentimental Journey*, ed. Gardner D. Stout, Jr. [Berkeley: University of California Press, 1967], p. 273).

sorrow and unkindness—still nature will prevail—and if I blush at recollecting past enjoyment, it is the rosy hue of pleasure heightened by modesty; for the blush of modesty and shame are as distinct as the emotions by which they are produced.

I need scarcely inform you, after telling you of my walks, that my constitution has been renovated here; and that I have recovered my activity, even whilst attaining a little *embonpoint.* My imprudence last winter, and some untoward accidents just at the time I was weaning my child, had reduced me to a state of weakness which I never before experienced.[2] A slow fever preyed on me every night, during my residence in Sweden, and after I arrived at Tonsberg. By chance I found a fine rivulet filtered through the rocks, and confined in a bason for the cattle. It tasted to me like a chalybeat;[3] at any rate it was pure; and the good effect of the various waters which invalids are sent to drink, depends, I believe, more on the air, exercise and change of scene, than on their medicinal qualities. I therefore determined to turn my morning walks towards it, and seek for health from the nymph of the fountain; partaking of the beverage offered to the tenants of the shade.

Chance likewise led me to discover a new pleasure, equally beneficial to my health. I wished to avail myself of my vicinity to the sea, and bathe; but it was not possible near the town; there was no convenience. The young woman whom I mentioned to you, proposed

---

2. See *The Love Letters of Mary Wollstonecraft to Gilbert Imlay,* ed. Roger Ingpen (Philadelphia: 1908), especially Letter XXXII (9 January 1795) and XXXIV (30 January 1795). Wollstonecraft had weaned Fanny on the advice of friends who thought doing so would improve her health, but they "did not know that the canker-worm was at work at the core" (p. 81).

3. A *chalybeate* is mineral or spring water taken as a tonic.

rowing me across the water, amongst the rocks; but as she was pregnant, I insisted on taking one of the oars, and learning to row. It was not difficult; and I do not know a pleasanter exercise. I soon became expert, and my train of thinking kept time, as it were, with the oars, or I suffered the boat to be carried along by the current, indulging a pleasing forgetfulness, or fallacious hopes. —How fallacious! yet, without hope, what is to sustain life, but the fear of annihilation—the only thing of which I have ever felt a dread—I cannot bear to think of being no more—of losing myself—though existence is often but a painful consciousness of misery; nay, it appears to me impossible that I should cease to exist, or that this active, restless spirit, equally alive to joy and sorrow, should only be organized dust—ready to fly abroad the moment the spring snaps, or the spark goes out, which kept it together. Surely something resides in this heart that is not perishable—and life is more than a dream.

Sometimes, to take up my oar, once more, when the sea was calm, I was amused by disturbing the innumerable young star fish which floated just below the surface: I had never observed them before; for they have not a hard shell, like those which I have seen on the sea-shore. They look like thickened water, with a white edge; and four purple circles, of different forms, were in the middle, over an incredible number of fibres, or white lines. Touching them, the cloudy substance would turn or close, first on one side, then on the other, very gracefully; but when I took one of them up in the ladle with which I heaved the water out of the boat, it appeared only a colourless jelly.

I did not see any of the seals, numbers of which followed our boat when we landed in Sweden; for though I like to sport in the water, I should have had no desire to join in their gambols.

Enough, you will say, of inanimate nature, and of brutes, to use the lordly phrase of man; let me hear something of the inhabitants.

The gentleman with whom I had business, is the mayor of Tonsberg; he speaks English intelligibly; and, having a sound understanding, I was sorry that his numerous occupations prevented my gaining as much information from him as I could have drawn forth, had we frequently conversed. The people of the town, as far as I had an opportunity of knowing their sentiments, are extremely well satisfied with his manner of discharging his office. He has a degree of information and good sense which excites respect, whilst a chearfulness, almost amounting to gaiety, enables him to reconcile differences, and keep his neighbours in good humour. —"I lost my horse," said a woman to me; "but ever since, when I want to send to the mill, or go out, the mayor lends me one. —He scolds if I do not come for it."

A criminal was branded, during my stay here, for the third offence; but the relief he received made him declare that the judge was one of the best men in the world.

I sent this wretch a trifle, at different times, to take with him into slavery. As it was more than he expected, he wished very much to see me; and this wish brought to my remembrance an anecdote I heard when I was in Lisbon.[4]

---

4. Wollstonecraft had been in Lisbon in 1785 to nurse her friend Fanny Blood Skeys (see Letter VI, note 7), and she stayed on a few weeks after Fanny's death.

A wretch who had been imprisoned several years, during which period lamps had been put up, was at last condemned to a cruel death; yet, in his way to execution, he only wished for one night's respite, to see the city lighted.

Having dined in company at the mayor's, I was invited with his family to spend the day at one of the richest merchant's houses. —Though I could not speak Danish, I knew that I could see a great deal: yes; I am persuaded that I have formed a very just opinion of the character of the Norwegians, without being able to hold converse with them.

I had expected to meet some company; yet was a little disconcerted at being ushered into an apartment full of well-dressed people; and, glancing my eyes round, they rested on several very pretty faces. Rosy cheeks, sparkling eyes, and light brown or golden locks; for I never saw so much hair with a yellow cast; and, with their fine complexions, it looked very becoming.

These women seem a mixture of indolence and vivacity; they scarcely ever walk out, and were astonished that I should, for pleasure; yet they are immoderately fond of dancing. Unaffected in their manners, if they have no pretensions to elegance, simplicity often produces a gracefulness of deportment, when they are animated by a particular desire to please—which was the case at present. The solitariness of my situation, which they thought terrible, interested them very much in my favour. They gathered round me—sung to me—and one of the prettiest, to whom I gave my hand, with some degree of cordiality, to meet the glance of her eyes, kissed me very affectionately.

At dinner, which was conducted with great hospitality, though we remained at table too long, they sung several songs, and, amongst the rest, translations of some patriotic French ones. As the evening advanced, they became playful, and we kept up a sort of conversation of gestures. As their minds were totally uncultivated, I did not lose much, perhaps gained, by not being able to understand them; for fancy probably filled up, more to their advantage, the void in the picture. Be that as it may, they excited my sympathy; and I was very much flattered when I was told, the next day, that they said it was a pleasure to look at me, I appeared so good-natured.

The men were generally captains of ships. Several spoke English very tolerably; but they were merely matter of fact men, confined to a very narrow circle of observation. I found it difficult to obtain from them any information respecting their own country, when the fumes of tobacco did not keep me at a distance.

I was invited to partake of some other feasts, and always had to complain of the quantity of provision, and the length of time taken to consume it; for it would not have been proper to have said devour, all went on so fair and softly. The servants wait as slowly as their mistresses carve.

The young women here, as well as in Sweden, have commonly bad teeth, which I attribute to the same causes. They are fond of finery, but do not pay the necessary attention to their persons, to render beauty less transient than a flower; and that interesting expression which sentiment and accomplishments give, seldom supplies its place.

The servants have likewise an inferior sort of food here; but their masters are not allowed to strike them with impunity. I might have added mistresses; for it was a complaint of this kind, brought before the mayor, which led me to a knowledge of the fact.

The wages are low, which is particularly unjust, because the price of clothes is much higher than provisions. A young woman, who is wet nurse to the mistress of the inn where I lodge, receives only twelve dollars a year, and pays ten for the nursing of her own child; the father had run away to get clear of the expense. There was something in this most painful state of widowhood which excited my compassion, and led me to reflections on the instability of the most flattering plans of happiness, that were painful in the extreme, till I was ready to ask whether this world was not created to exhibit every possible combination of wretchedness. I asked these questions of a heart writhing with anguish, whilst I listened to a melancholy ditty sung by this poor girl. It was too early for thee to be abandoned, thought I, and I hastened out of the house, to take my solitary evening's walk—And here I am again, to talk of any thing, but the pangs arising from the discovery of estranged affection, and the lonely sadness of a deserted heart.

The father and mother, if the father can be ascertained, are obliged to maintain an illegitimate child at their joint expense; but, should the father disappear, go up the country or to sea, the mother must maintain it herself. However, accidents of this kind do not prevent their marrying; and then it is not unusual to take the child or children home; and they are brought up very amicably with the marriage progeny.

I took some pains to learn what books were written originally in their language; but for any certain information respecting the state of Danish literature, I must wait till I arrive at Copenhagen.

The sound of the language is soft, a great proportion of the words ending in vowels; and there is a simplicity in the turn of some of the phrases which have been translated to me, that pleased and interested me. In the country, the farmers use the *thou* and *thee;* and they do not acquire the polite plurals of the towns by meeting at market. The not having markets established in the large towns appears to me a great inconvenience. When the farmers have any thing to sell, they bring it to the neighbouring town, and take it from house to house. I am surprised that the inhabitants do not feel how very incommodious this usage is to both parties, and redress it. They indeed perceive it; for when I have introduced the subject, they acknowledged that they were often in want of necessaries, there being no butchers, and they were often obliged to buy what they did not want; yet it was the *custom;* and the changing of customs of a long standing requires more energy than they yet possess. I received a similar reply, when I attempted to persuade the women that they injured their children by keeping them too warm. The only way of parrying off my reasoning was, that they must do as other people did. In short, reason on any subject of change, and they stop you by saying that "the town would talk." A person of sense, with a large fortune, to insure respect, might be very useful here, by inducing them to treat their children, and manage their sick properly, and eat food dressed in a simpler manner: the example, for instance, of a count's lady.

Reflecting on these prejudices made me revert to the wisdom of those legislators who established institutions for the good of the body, under the pretext of serving heaven for the salvation of the soul. These might with strict propriety be termed pious frauds; and I admire the Peruvian pair for asserting that they came from the sun, when their conduct proved that they meant to enlighten a benighted country, whose obedience, or even attention, could only be secured by awe.[5]

Thus much for conquering the *inertia* of reason; but, when it is once in motion, fables, once held sacred, may be ridiculed; and sacred they were, when useful to mankind. —Prometheus alone stole fire to animate the first man; his posterity need not supernatural aid to preserve the species, though love is generally termed a flame; and it may not be necessary much longer to suppose men inspired by heaven to inculcate the duties which demand special grace, when reason convinces them that they are the happiest who are the most nobly employed.

In a few days I am to set out for the western part of Norway, and then shall return by land to Gothenburg. I cannot think of leaving this place without regret. I speak of the place before the inhabitants, though there is a tenderness in their artless kindness which attaches me to them; but it is an attachment that inspires a regret very different from that I felt at leaving Hull, in my way to Sweden. The domestic happiness, and goodhumoured gaiety, of the amiable family where I and my Frances were so hospitably received, would have been

---

5. The "Peruvian pair" may be a reference to the Inca of Peru and his lovely daughter Orazia in John Dryden and Robert Howard's *The Indian Queen* (1663). The Inca desires to reward his conquering marshall, the Mexican Montezuma, with land, but when Montezuma requests Orazia's hand, the Inca responds, "Thou deserv'st to die./ O thou great author of our progeny,/ Thou glorious sun, dost thou not blush to shine,/ While such base blood attempts to mix with thine!" (I.i.47–50). Wollstonecraft may have known either the play or Henry Purcell's operatic version, the last scene of which is set in the Temple of the Sun.

sufficient to insure the tenderest remembrance, without the recollection of the social evenings to stimulate it, when good-breeding gave dignity to sympathy, and wit, zest to reason.

Adieu! —I am just informed that my horse has been waiting this quarter of an hour. I now venture to ride out alone. The steeple serves as a land-mark. I once or twice lost my way, walking alone, without being able to inquire after a path. I was therefore obliged to make to the steeple, or wind-mill, over hedge and ditch.

Your's truly.

LETTER IX

I HAVE already informed you that there are only two noblemen who have estates of any magnitude in Norway. One of these has a house near Tonsberg, at which he has not resided for some years, having been at court, or on embassies. He is now the Danish ambassador in London. The house is pleasantly situated, and the grounds about it fine; but their neglected appearance plainly tells that there is nobody at home.

A stupid kind of sadness, to my eye, always reigns in a huge habitation where only servants live to put cases on the furniture and open the windows. I enter as I would into the tomb of the Capulets, to look at the family pictures that here frown in armour, or smile in ermine. The mildew respects not the lordly robe; and the worm riots unchecked on the cheek of beauty.

There was nothing in the architecture of the building, or the form of the furniture, to detain me from the avenue where the aged pines stretched along majestically. Time had given a greyish cast to their ever-green foliage; and they stood, like sires of the forest, sheltered on all sides by a rising progeny. I had not ever seen so many oaks together in Norway, as in these woods, nor such large aspens as here were agitated by the breeze, rendering the wind audible—nay, musical; for melody seemed on the wing around me. How different was the fresh odour that re-animated me in the avenue, from the damp chillness of the apartments; and as little did the gloomy thoughtfulness excited by the dusty hangings, and worm-eaten pictures, resemble the reveries inspired by the soothing melancholy of their shade. In the winter, these august pines, towering above the snow, must relieve the eye beyond measure, and give life to the white waste.

The continual recurrence of pine and fir groves, in the day, sometimes wearies the sight; but, in the evening, nothing can be more picturesque, or, more properly speaking, better calculated to produce poetical images. Passing through them, I have been struck with a mystic kind of reverence, and I did, as it were, homage to their venerable shadows. Not nymphs, but philosophers, seemed to inhabit them—ever musing; I could scarcely conceive that they were without some consciousness of existence—without a calm enjoyment of the pleasure they diffused.

How often do my feelings produce ideas that remind me of the origin of many poetical fictions. In solitude, the imagination bodies forth its conceptions unrestrained, and stops enraptured to adore the beings of its own creation. These are moments of bliss; and the memory recals them with delight.

But I have almost forgotten the matters of fact I meant to relate, respecting the counts. They have the presentation of the livings on their estates, appoint the judges, and different civil officers, the crown reserving to itself the privilege of sanctioning them. But, though they appoint, they cannot dismiss. Their tenants also occupy their farms for life, and are obliged to obey any summons to work on the part he reserves for himself; but they are paid for their labour. In short, I have seldom heard of any noblemen so innoxious.

Observing that the gardens round the count's estate were better cultivated than any I had before seen, I was led to reflect on the advantages which naturally accrue from the feudal tenures. The tenants of the count are obliged to work at a stated price, in his grounds and garden; and the instruction which they imperceptibly receive from the head gardener, tends to render them useful, and makes them, in the common course of things, better husbandmen and gardeners on their own little farms. Thus the great, who alone travel, in this period of society, for the observation of manners and customs made by sailors is very confined, bring home improvement to promote their own comfort, which is gradually spread abroad amongst the people, till they are stimulated to think for themselves.

The bishops have not large revenues; and the priests are appointed by the king before they come to them to be ordained. There is commonly some little farm annexed to the parsonage; and the inhabitants subscribe voluntarily, three times a year, in addition to the church fees, for the support of the clergyman. The church lands were seized when lutheranism was introduced; the desire of obtaining them being probably the real stimulus of reformation. The tithes, which are never required in kind, are divided into three parts; one to the king, another to the incumbent, and the third to repair the delapidations of the parsonage. They do not amount to much. And the stipend allowed to the different civil officers is also too small, scarcely deserving to be termed an independence; that of the custom-house officers is not sufficient to procure the necessaries of life—no wonder, then, if necessity leads them to knavery. Much public virtue cannot be expected till every employment, putting perquisites out of the question, has a salary sufficient to reward industry, whilst none are so great as to permit the possessor to remain idle. It is this want of proportion between profit and labour which debases men, producing the sycophantic appellations of patron and client; and that pernicious *esprit du corps*, proverbially vicious.

The farmers are hospitable, as well as independent. Offering once to pay for some coffee I drank when taking shelter from the rain, I was asked, rather angrily, if a little coffee was worth paying for. They smoke, and drink drams; but not so much as formerly. Drunkenness, often the attendant disgrace of hospitality, will here, as well as every where else, give place to gallantry and refinement of manners; but the change will not be suddenly produced.

The people of every class are constant in their attendance at church; they are very fond of dancing: and the Sunday evenings in Norway, as in catholic countries, are spent in exercises which exhilerate the spirits, without vitiating the heart. The rest of labour ought to be gay; and the gladness I have felt in France on a Sunday, or decadi,[1] which I caught from the faces around me, was a sentiment more truly religious than all the stupid stillness which the streets of London ever inspired where the sabbath is so decorously observed. I recollect, in the country parts of England the churchwardens used to go out, during the service, to see if they could

---

1. During the French Revolution, by action of the Convention in October 1793, each month was divided into three *décades*, and the *décadi* was the tenth and last day of this new week.

catch any luckless wight playing at bowls or skittles; yet what could be more harmless? It would even, I think, be a great advantage to the English, if feats of activity, I do not include boxing matches, were encouraged on a Sunday, as it might stop the progress of methodism, and of that fanatical spirit which appears to be gaining ground. I was surprised when I visited Yorkshire, in my way to Sweden, to find that sullen narrowness of thinking had made such a progress since I was an inhabitant of the country. I could hardly have supposed that sixteen or seventeen years could have produced such an alteration for the worse in the morals of a place; yes, I say morals; for observance of forms, and avoiding of practices, indifferent in themselves, often supplies the place of that regular attention to duties which are so natural, that they seldom are vauntingly exercised, though they are worth all the precepts of the law and the prophets. Besides, many of these deluded people, with the best meaning, actually lose their reason, and become miserable, the dread of damnation throwing them into a state which merits the term: and still more, in running after their preachers, expecting to promote their salvation, they disregard their welfare in this world, and neglect the interest and comfort of their families: so that in proportion as they attain a reputation for piety, they become idle.

Aristocracy and fanaticism seem equally to be gaining ground in England, particularly in the place I have mentioned: I saw very little of either in Norway. The people are regular in their attendance on public worship; but religion does not interfere with their employments.

As the farmers cut away the wood, they clear the ground. Every year, therefore, the country is becoming fitter to support the inhabitants. Half a century ago the Dutch, I am told, only paid for the cutting down of the wood, and the farmers were glad to get rid of it without giving themselves any trouble. At present they form a just estimate of its value; nay, I was surprised to find even fire wood so dear, when it appears to be in such plenty. The destruction, or gradual reduction, of their forests, will probably meliorate the climate; and their manners will naturally improve in the same ratio as industry requires ingenuity. It is very fortunate that men are, a long time, but just above the brute creation, or the greater part of the earth would never have been rendered habitable; because it is the patient labour of men, who are only seeking for a subsistence, which produces whatever embellishes existence, affording leisure for the cultivation of the arts and sciences, that lift man so far above his first state. I never, my friend, thought so deeply of the advantages obtained by human industry as since I have been in Norway. The world requires, I see, the hand of man to perfect it; and as this task naturally unfolds the faculties he exercises, it is physically impossible that he should have remained in Rousseau's golden age of stupidity.[2] And, considering

2. Wollstonecraft is ridiculing Jean Jacques Rousseau's concept of the "state of nature" which, he had suggested in his early works, was that ideal time in which humankind, untrammelled by institutions, could have been free and (an important corollary) solitary. Wollstonecraft, in *A Vindication of the Rights of Woman* (1792), had gone to some length to refute the idea of the "natural man," chiefly on the grounds that Rousseau's antisocial ideas reflect on God's wisdom. Rousseau said that God made the world good but that man introduced evil; Wollstonecraft thinks that such a theory implies divine short-sightedness at best. Nor does Wollstonecraft believe man is a solitary animal, for she insists that the establishment of a good society is the careful and rational process of constructing those public institutions consistent with individual liberty.

the question of human happiness, where, oh! where does it reside? Has it taken up its abode with unconscious ignorance, or with the high-wrought mind? Is it the offspring of thoughtless animal spirits, or the elve of fancy continually flitting round the expected pleasure? The increasing population of the earth must necessarily tend to its improvement, as the means of existence are multiplied by invention.

You have probably made similar reflections in America, where the face of the country, I suppose, resembles the wilds of Norway.[3] I am delighted with the romantic views I daily contemplate, animated by the purest air; and I am interested by the simplicity of manners which reigns around me. Still nothing so soon wearies out the feelings as unmarked simplicity. I am, therefore, half convinced, that I could not live very comfortably exiled from the countries where mankind are so much further advanced in knowledge, imperfect as it is, and unsatisfactory to the thinking mind. Even now I begin to long to hear what you are doing in England and France. My thoughts fly from this wilderness to the polished circles of the world, till recollecting its vices and follies, I bury myself in the woods, but find it necessary to emerge again, that I may not lose sight of the wisdom and virtue which exalts my nature.

What a long time it requires to know ourselves; and yet almost every one has more of this knowledge than he is willing to own, even to himself. I cannot immediately determine whether I ought to rejoice at having turned over in this solitude a new page in the history

3. Gilbert Imlay was from New Jersey and had traveled west to Kentucky. Wollstonecraft must have had a very imperfect conception of the terrain of eastern North America if she thought it resembled Norway.

of my own heart, though I may venture to assure you that a further acquaintance with mankind only tends to increase my respect for your judgment, and esteem for your character.

Farewell!

LETTER X

I HAVE once more, my friend, taken flight; for I left Tonsberg yesterday; but with an intention of returning, in my way back to Sweden.

The road to Laurvig is very fine, and the country the best cultivated in Norway. I never before admired the beech tree; and when I met stragglers here, they pleased me still less. Long and lank, they would have forced me to allow that the line of beauty requires some curves, if the stately pine, standing near, erect, throwing her vast arms around, had not looked beautiful, in opposition to such narrow rules.

In these respects my very reason obliges me to permit my feelings to be my criterion. Whatever excites emotion has charms for me; though I insist that the cultivation of the mind, by warming, nay almost creating the imagination, produces taste, and an immense variety of sensations and emotions, partaking of the exquisite pleasure inspired by beauty and sublimity. As I know of no end to them, the word infinite, so often misapplied, might, on this occasion, be introduced with something like propriety.

But I have rambled away again. I intended to have remarked to you the effect produced by a grove of towering beech. The airy lightness of their foliage admitting a degree of sunshine, which, giving a transparency to the leaves, exhibited an appearance of freshness and elegance that I had never before remarked, I thought of descriptions of Italian scenery. But these evanescent graces seemed the effect of enchantment; and I imperceptibly breathed softly, lest I should destroy what was real, yet looked so like the creation of fancy. Dryden's fable of the flower and the leaf was not a more poetical reverie.[1]

Adieu, however, to fancy, and to all the sentiments which ennoble our nature. I arrived at Laurvig, and found myself in the midst of a group of lawyers, of different descriptions. My head turned round, my heart grew sick, as I regarded visages deformed by vice; and listened to accounts of chicanery that were continually embroiling the ignorant. These locusts[2] will probably diminish, as the people become more enlightened. In this period of social life the commonalty are always cunningly attentive to their own interest; but their faculties, confined to a few objects, are so narrowed, that they cannot discover it in the general good. The profession of the law renders a set of men still shrewder and more selfish than the rest; and it is these men, whose wits have been sharpened by knavery, who here undermine morality, confounding right and wrong.

The count of Bernstorff, who really appears to me, from all I can gather, to have the good of the people

---

1. John Dryden's "The Flower and the Leaf: or The Lady in the Arbor; a vision (out of Chaucer)" (1700) is an allegorical poem which pits the transient flower of pleasure against the laurel leaf of ambition, "the sign of Labour crown'd."

2. Persons of destructive tendencies.

at heart, aware of this, has lately sent to the mayor of each district to name, according to the size of the place, four or six of the best-informed inhabitants, not men of the law, out of which the citizens were to elect two, who are to be termed *mediators*. Their office is to endeavour to prevent litigious suits, and conciliate differences. And no suit is to be commenced before the parties have discussed the dispute at their weekly meeting. If a reconciliation should, in consequence, take place, it is to be registered, and the parties are not allowed to retract.

By these means ignorant people will be prevented from applying for advice to men who may justly be termed stirrers-up of strife. They have, for a long time, to use a significant vulgarism, set the people by the ears, and lived by the spoil they caught up in the scramble. There is some reason to hope that this regulation will diminish their number, and restrain their mischievous activity. But till trials by jury are established, little justice can be expected in Norway. Judges who cannot be bribed are often timid, and afraid of offending bold knaves, lest they should raise a set of hornets about themselves. The fear of censure undermines all energy of character; and, labouring to be prudent, they lose sight of rectitude. Besides, nothing is left to their conscience, or sagacity; they must be governed by evidence, though internally convinced that it is false.

There is a considerable iron manufactory at Laurvig, for coarse work, and a lake near the town supplies the water necessary for working several mills belonging to it.

This establishment belongs to the count of Laurvig. Without a fortune, and influence equal to his, such a work could not have been set afloat; personal fortunes are not yet sufficient to support such undertakings; nevertheless the inhabitants of the town speak of the size of his estate as an evil, because it obstructs commerce. The occupiers of small farms are obliged to bring their wood to the neighbouring sea-ports, to be shipped; but he, wishing to increase the value of his, will not allow it to be thus gradually cut down; which turns the trade into another channel. Added to this, nature is against them, the bay being open and insecure. I could not help smiling when I was informed that in a hard gale a vessel had been wrecked in the main street. When there are such a number of excellent harbours on the coast, it is a pity that accident has made one of the largest towns grow up in a bad one.

The father of the present count was a distant relation of the family; he resided constantly in Denmark; and his son follows his example. They have not been in possession of the estate many years; and their predecessor lived near the town, introducing a degree of profligacy of manners which has been ruinous to the inhabitants in every respect, their fortunes not being equal to the prevailing extravagance.

What little I have seen of the manners of the people does not please me so well as those of Tonsberg. I am forewarned that I shall find them still more cunning and fraudulent as I advance towards the westward, in proportion as traffic takes place of agriculture; for their towns are built on naked rocks; the streets are narrow bridges; and the inhabitants are all seafaring men, or owners of ships, who keep shops.

The inn I was at in Laurvig, this journey, was not the same that I was at before. It is a good one; the people civil, and the accommodations decent. They seem to be better provided in Sweden; but in justice I ought to add, that they charge more extravagantly. My bill at Tonsberg was also much higher than I had paid in Sweden, and much higher than it ought to have been where provisions are so cheap. Indeed they seem to consider foreigners as strangers whom they should never see again, and might fairly pluck. And the inhabitants of the western coast, insulated, as it were, regard those of the east almost as strangers. Each town in that quarter seems to be a great family, suspicious of every other, allowing none to cheat them, but themselves; and, right or wrong, they support one another in the face of justice.

On this journey I was fortunate enough to have one companion with more enlarged views than the generality of his countrymen, who spoke English tolerably.

I was informed that we might still advance a mile and a quarter in our *cabrioles;*[3] afterwards there was no choice, but of a single horse and wretched path, or a boat, the usual mode of travelling.

We therefore sent our baggage forward in the boat, and followed rather slowly, for the road was rocky and sandy. We passed, however, through several beech groves, which still delighted me by the freshness of their light green foliage, and the elegance of their assemblage, forming retreats to veil, without obscuring the sun.

I was surprised, at approaching the water, to find a little cluster of houses pleasantly situated, and an excellent inn. I could have wished to have remained there all night; but as the wind was fair, and the evening fine, I was afraid to trust to the wind, the uncertain wind of to-morrow. We therefore left Helgeraac immediately, with the declining sun.

---

3. A small carriage; see Letter VI, note 4.

Though we were in the open sea, we sailed more amongst the rocks and islands than in my passage from Stromstad; and they often formed very picturesque combinations. Few of the high ridges were entirely bare; the seeds of some pines or firs had been wafted by the winds or waves, and they stood to brave the elements.

Sitting then in a little boat on the ocean, amidst strangers, with sorrow and care pressing hard on me,—buffeting me about from clime to clime,—I felt

"Like the lone shrub at random cast,
That sighs and trembles at each blast!"4

On some of the largest rocks there were actually groves, the retreat of foxes and hares, which, I suppose, had tript over the ice during the winter, without thinking to regain the main land before the thaw.

Several of the islands were inhabited by pilots; and the Norwegian pilots are allowed to be the best in the world; perfectly acquainted with their coast, and ever at hand to observe the first signal or sail. They pay a small tax to the king, and to the regulating officer, and enjoy the fruit of their indefatigable industry.

One of the islands, called Virgin Land, is a flat, with some depth of earth, extending for half a Norwegian mile, with three farms on it, tolerably well cultivated.

On some of the bare rocks I saw straggling houses; they rose above the denomination of huts inhabited by fishermen. My companions assured me that they were very comfortable dwellings, and that they have not only the necessaries, but even what might be reckoned the superfluities of life. It was too late for me to go on

4. I have been unable to locate the source of this quotation.

shore, if you will allow me to give that name to shivering rocks, to ascertain the fact.

But rain coming on, and the night growing dark, the pilot declared that it would be dangerous for us to attempt to go to the place of our destination, *East Riisoer*, a Norwegian mile and a half further; and we determined to stop for the night at a little haven; some half dozen houses scattered under the curve of a rock. Though it became darker and darker, our pilot avoided the blind rocks with great dexterity.

It was about ten o'clock when we arrived; and the old hostess quickly prepared me a comfortable bed—a little too soft, or so; but I was weary; and opening the window to admit the sweetest of breezes to fan me to sleep, I sunk into the most luxurious rest: it was more than refreshing. The hospitable sprites of the grots surely hovered round my pillow; and if I woke, it was to listen to the melodious whispering of the wind amongst them, or to feel the mild breath of morn. Light slumbers produced dreams, where Paradise was before me. My little cherub was again hiding her face in my bosom. I heard her sweet cooing beat on my heart from the cliffs, and saw her tiny footsteps on the sands. New-born hopes seemed, like the rainbow, to appear in the clouds of sorrow, faint, yet sufficient to amuse away despair.

Some refreshing but heavy showers have detained us; and here I am writing quite alone—something more than gay, for which I want a name.

I could almost fancy myself in Nootka Sound,[5] or on some of the islands on the north west coast of America.

---

5. Specifically, a sound into Vancouver Island, off Western Canada, but perhaps used by Wollstonecraft to indicate the whole series of inlets or *fjords* reaching into Vancouver Island.

We entered by a narrow pass through the rocks, which from this abode appear more romantic than you can well imagine; and seal-skins, hanging at the door to dry, add to the illusion.

It is indeed a corner of the world; but you would be surprised to see the cleanliness and comfort of the dwelling. The shelves are not only shining with pewter and queen's ware,[6] but some articles in silver, more ponderous, it is true, than elegant. The linen is good, as well as white. All the females spin; and there is a loom in the kitchen. A sort of individual taste appeared in the arrangement of the furniture (this is not the place for imitation), and a kindness in their desire to oblige—how superior to the apish politeness of the towns! where the people, affecting to be well bred, fatigue with their endless ceremony.

The mistress is a widow; her daughter is married to a pilot, and has three cows. They have a little patch of land at about the distance of two English miles, where they make hay for the winter, which they bring home in a boat. They live here very cheap, getting money from the vessels which stress of weather, or other causes, bring into their harbour. I suspect, by their furniture, that they smuggle a little. I can now credit the account of the other houses, which I last night thought exaggerated.

I have been conversing with one of my companions respecting the laws and regulations of Norway. He is a man with a great portion of common sense, and heart, —yes, a warm heart. This is not the first time I have remarked heart without sentiment: they are distinct. The former depends on the rectitude of the feelings, on

---

6. A kind of pottery or stoneware.

truth of sympathy: these characters have more tenderness than passion; the latter has a higher source; call it
imagination, genius, or what you will, it is something
very different. I have been laughing with these simple,
worthy *folk*, to give you one of my half score Danish
words, and letting as much of my heart flow out in
sympathy as they can take. Adieu! I must trip up the
rocks. The rain is over. Let me catch pleasure on the
wing—I may be melancholy to-morrow. Now all my
nerves keep time with the melody of nature. Ah! let me
be happy whilst I can. The tear starts as I think of it. I
must fly from thought, and find refuge from sorrow in
a strong imagination—the only solace for a feeling heart.
Phantoms of bliss! ideal forms of excellence! again in-
close me in your magic circle, and wipe clear from my
remembrance the disappointments which render the
sympathy painful, which experience rather increases
than damps; by giving the indulgence of feeling the
sanction of reason.

Once more farewell!

LETTER XI

I LEFT Portoer, the little haven I mentioned, soon after I finished my last letter. The sea was rough; and I perceived that our pilot was right not to venture farther during a hazy night. We had agreed to pay four dollars[2] for a boat from Helgeraac. I mention the sum, because they would demand twice as much from a stranger. I was obliged to pay fifteen for the one I hired at Stromstad. When we were ready to set out, our boatman offered to return a dollar, and let us go in one of the boats of the place, the pilot who lived there being better acquainted with the coast. He only demanded a dollar and half, which was reasonable. I found him a civil and rather intelligent man: he was in the American service several years, during the revolution.

I soon perceived that an experienced mariner was necessary to guide us; for we were continually obliged to tack about, to avoid the rocks, which, scarcely reaching to the surface of the water, could only be discovered by the breaking of the waves over them.

---

1. From Wollstonecraft's Supplementary Note (pp. 199–200) it is clear that "dollar" here means "rixdollar," and at that time the rate of exchange was five rixdollars to £1 British sterling.

The view of this wild coast, as we sailed along it, afforded me a continual subject for meditation. I anticipated the future improvement of the world, and observed how much man had still to do, to obtain of the earth all it could yield. I even carried my speculations so far as to advance a million or two of years to the moment when the earth would perhaps be so perfectly cultivated, and so completely peopled, as to render it necessary to inhabit every spot; yes; these bleak shores. Imagination went still farther, and pictured the state of man when the earth could no longer support him. Where was he to fly to from universal famine? Do not smile: I really became distressed for these fellow creatures, yet unborn. The images fastened on me, and the world appeared a vast prison. I was soon to be in a smaller one—for no other name can I give to Rusoer. It would be difficult to form an idea of the place, if you have never seen one of these rocky coasts.

We were a considerable time entering amongst the islands, before we saw about two hundred houses crowded together, under a very high rock—still higher appearing above. Talk not of bastilles! To be born here, was to be bastilled by nature—shut out from all that opens the understanding, or enlarges the heart. Huddled one behind another, not more than a quarter of the dwellings even had a prospect of the sea. A few planks formed passages from house to house, which you must often scale, mounting steps like a ladder, to enter.

The only road across the rocks leads to a habitation, sterile enough, you may suppose, when I tell you that the little earth on the adjacent ones was carried there by the late inhabitant. A path, almost impracticable for a horse, goes on to Arendall, still further to the westward.

I enquired for a walk, and mounting near two hundred steps made round a rock, walked up and down for about a hundred yards, viewing the sea, to which I quickly descended by steps that cheated the declivity. The ocean, and these tremendous bulwarks, enclosed me on every side. I felt the confinement, and wished for wings to reach still loftier cliffs, whose slippery sides no foot was so hardy as to tread; yet what was it to see? —only a boundless waste of water—not a glimpse of smiling nature—not a patch of lively green to relieve the aching sight, or vary the objects of meditation.

I felt my breath oppressed, though nothing could be clearer than the atmosphere. Wandering there alone, I found the solitude desirable; my mind was stored with ideas, which this new scene associated with astonishing rapidity. But I shuddered at the thought of receiving existence, and remaining here, in the solitude of ignorance, till forced to leave a world of which I had seen so little; for the character of the inhabitants is as uncultivated, if not as picturesquely wild, as their abode.

Having no employment but traffic, of which a contraband trade makes the basis of their profit, the coarsest feelings of honesty are quickly blunted. You may suppose that I speak in general terms; and that, with all the disadvantages of nature and circumstances, there are still some respectable exceptions, the more praiseworthy, as tricking is a very contagious mental disease that dries up all the generous juices of the heart. Nothing genial, in fact, appears around this place, or within the circle of its rocks. And, now I recollect, it seems to me that the most genial and humane characters I have met with in life, were most alive to the sentiments inspired by tranquil country scenes. What, indeed, is to humanise these beings, who rest shut up, for they seldom even open their windows, smoaking, drinking brandy, and driving bargains? I have been almost stifled by these smoakers. They begin in the morning, and are rarely without their pipe till they go to bed. Nothing can be more disgusting than the rooms and men towards the evening: breath, teeth, clothes, and furniture, all are spoilt. It is well that the women are not very delicate, or they would only love their husbands because they were their husbands. Perhaps, you may add, that the remark need not be confined to so small a part of the world; and, *entre nous*, I am of the same opinion. You must not term this inuendo fancy, for it does not come home.[2]

If I had not determined to write, I should have found my confinement here, even for three or four days, tedious. I have no books; and to pace up and down a small room, looking at tiles, overhung by rocks, soon becomes wearisome. I cannot mount two hundred steps, to walk a hundred yards, many times in the day. Besides, the rocks, retaining the heat of the sun, are intolerably warm. I am nevertheless very well; for though there is a shrewdness in the character of these people, depraved by a sordid love of money which repels me, still the comparisons they force me to make keep my heart calm, by exercising my understanding.

Every where wealth commands too much respect; but here, almost exclusively; and it is the only object pursued—not through brake and briar,[3] but over rocks

---

2. A paraphrase of this sentence might read, "Do not think that I am here capriciously insinuating your behavior towards me, since what I'm suggesting does not touch you." Wollstonecraft considered Imlay her husband, and this is a delicate way of saying that she finds him attractive: i.e., she does not love him only because he is her husband.

3. See William Cowper, "The Needless Alarm," line 6: "That he [the squire] may follow them [the foxes] through brake and briar."

and waves—yet of what use would riches be to me? I have sometimes asked myself, were I confined to live in such a spot. I could only relieve a few distressed objects, perhaps render them idle, and all the rest of life would be a blank.

My present journey has given fresh force to my opinion, that no place is so disagreeable and unimproving as a country town. I should like to divide my time between the town and country; in a lone house, with the business of farming and planting, where my mind would gain strength by solitary musing; and in a metropolis to rub off the rust of thought, and polish the taste which the contemplation of nature had rendered just. Thus do we wish as we float down the stream of life, whilst chance does more to gratify a desire of knowledge than our best-laid plans. A degree of exertion, produced by some want, more or less painful, is probably the price we must all pay for knowledge. How few authors or artists have arrived at eminence who have not lived by their employment?

I was interrupted yesterday by business, and was prevailed upon to dine with the English vice-consul. His house being open to the sea, I was more at large; and the hospitality of the table pleased me, though the bottle was rather too freely pushed about. Their manner of entertaining was such as I have frequently remarked when I have been thrown in the way of people without education, who have more money than wit, that is, than they know what to do with. The women were unaffected, but had not the natural grace which was often conspicuous at Tonsberg. There was even a striking difference in their dress; these having loaded themselves with finery, in the style of the sailors' girls of Hull or Portsmouth. Taste has not yet taught them to make any but an ostentatious display of wealth: yet I could perceive even here the first steps of the improvement which I am persuaded will make a very obvious progress in the course of half a century; and it ought not to be sooner, to keep pace with the cultivation of the earth. Improving manners will introduce finer moral feelings. They begin to read translations of some of the most useful German productions lately published; and one of our party sung a song, ridiculing the powers coalesced against France, and the company drank confusion to those who had dismembered Poland.[4]

The evening was extremely calm and beautiful. Not being able to walk, I requested a boat, as the only means of enjoying free air.

The view of the town was now extremely fine. A huge rocky mountain stood up behind it; and a vast cliff stretched on each side, forming a semicircle. In a recess of the rocks was a clump of pines, amongst which a steeple rose picturesquely beautiful.

The church-yard is almost the only verdant spot in the place. Here, indeed, friendship extends beyond the grave; and, to grant a sod of earth, is to accord a favour. I should rather chuse, did it admit of a choice, to sleep in some of the caves of the rocks; for I am become better reconciled to them since I climbed their craggy sides, last night, listening to the finest echoes I ever heard. We had a French-horn[5] with us; and there was

---

4. There had been two partitions of Poland, one in 1772 and one in 1793, redistributing large portions of its territory to Austria, Prussia, and Russia; in 1795 the Poles were fighting to regain their territory under famous revolutionary leaders like Kosciusko, but they were defeated. Poland was again to be partitioned in 1796.

5. The end-blown horn remained a hunting horn until the mid-eighteenth century, and in Scandinavia at this time a French horn might well have been a short animal horn with fingerholes. It was used by hunters and shepherds, and possibly even by sailors to announce a boat's arrival.

an enchanting wildness in the dying away of the rever-
beration, that quickly transported me to Shakspeare's
magic island.[6] Spirits unseen seemed to walk abroad,
and flit from cliff to cliff, to sooth my soul to peace.

I reluctantly returned to supper, to be shut up in a
warm room, only to view the vast shadows of the rocks
extending on the slumbering waves. I stood at the window some time before a buzz filled the drawing-room;
and now and then the dashing of a solitary oar rendered
the scene still more solemn.

Before I came here, I could scarcely have imagined
that a simple object, rocks, could have admitted of so
many interesting combinations—always grand, and often sublime.

Good night! God bless you!

---

6. Probably the island in *The Tempest* in which Prospero and Miranda
were shipwrecked, the dwelling place of the sprite Ariel.

LETTER XII

I LEFT East Rusoer the day before yesterday. The weather was very fine; but so calm that we loitered on the water near fourteen hours, only to make about six and twenty miles.

It seemed to me a sort of emancipation when we landed at Helgeraac. The confinement which every where struck me whilst sojourning amongst the rocks, made me hail the earth as a land of promise; and the situation shone with fresh lustre from the contrast—from appearing to be a free abode. Here it was possible to travel by land—I never thought this a comfort before, and my eyes, fatigued by the sparkling of the sun on the water, now contentedly reposed on the green expanse, half persuaded that such verdant meads had never till then regaled them.

I rose early to pursue my journey to Tonsberg. The country still wore a face of joy—and my soul was alive to its charms. Leaving the most lofty, and romantic of the cliffs behind us, we were almost continually descending to Tonsberg, through elysian scenes; for not only the sea, but mountains, rivers, lakes, and groves, gave an almost endless variety to the prospect. The cottagers were still leading home the hay; and the cottages, on this road, looked very comfortable. Peace and plenty—I mean not abundance, seemed to reign around —still I grew sad as I drew near my old abode. I was sorry to see the sun so high; it was broad noon. Tonsberg was something like a home—yet I was to enter without lighting-up pleasure in any eye—I dreaded the solitariness of my apartment, and wished for night to hide the starting tears, or to shed them on my pillow, and close my eyes on a world where I was destined to wander alone. Why has nature so many charms for me —calling forth and cherishing refined sentiments, only to wound the breast that fosters them? How illusive, perhaps the most so, are the plans of happiness founded on virtue and principle; what inlets of misery do they not open in a half civilized society? The satisfaction arising from conscious rectitude, will not calm an injured heart, when tenderness is ever finding excuses; and self-applause is a cold solitary feeling, that cannot supply the place of disappointed affection, without throwing a gloom over every prospect, which, banishing pleasure, does not exclude pain. I reasoned and reasoned; but my heart was two[1] full to allow me to remain in the house, and I walked, till I was wearied out, to purchase rest—or rather forgetfulness.

Employment has beguiled this day, and tomorrow I set out for Moss, in my way to Stromstad. At Gothenburg I shall embrace my *Fannikin;* probably she will not know me again—and I shall be hurt if she do not. How childish is this! still it is a natural feeling. I would not permit myself to indulge the "thick coming

---

1. Wollstonecraft means "too."

fears"[2] of fondness, whilst I was detained by business. —Yet I never saw a calf bounding in a meadow, that did not remind me of my little frolicker. A calf, you say. Yes; but a *capital* one, I own.

I cannot write composedly—I am every instant sinking into reveries—my heart flutters, I know not why. Fool! It is time thou wert at rest.

Friendship and domestic happiness are continually praised; yet how little is there of either in the world, because it requires more cultivation of mind to keep awake affection, even in our own hearts, than the common run of people suppose. Besides, few like to be seen as they really are; and a degree of simplicity, and of undisguised confidence, which, to uninterested observers, would almost border on weakness, is the charm, nay the essence of love or friendship: all the bewitching graces of childhood again appearing. As objects merely to exercise my taste, I therefore like to see people together who have an affection for each other; every turn of their features touches me, and remains pictured on my imagination in indelible characters. The zest of novelty is, however, necessary to rouse the languid sympathies which have been hacknied in the world; as is the factitious behaviour, falsely termed good-breeding, to amuse those, who, defective in taste, continually rely for pleasure on their animal spirits, which not being maintained by the imagination, are unavoidably sooner exhausted than the sentiments of the heart. Friendship is in general sincere at the commencement, and lasts whilst there is any thing to support it; but as a mixture of novelty and vanity is the usual prop, no wonder if it fall with the slender stay. The fop in the play, payed

---

2. *Macbeth* V.iii.38: "She is troubled with thick-coming fancies."

a greater compliment than he was aware of, when he said to a person, whom he meant to flatter, "I like you almost as well as a *new acquaintance.*"3 Why am I talking of friendship, after which I have had such a wild-goose chace. —I thought only of telling you that the crows, as well as wild-geese, are here birds of passage.4

---

3. In William Wycherley's *The Country Wife,* III.ii.166–67 Sparkish says to Harcourt, "For though I have known thee a great while, never go, if I do not love thee as well as a new acquaintance."

4. "Birds of passage" are those which migrate seasonally.

LETTER XIII

I LEFT Tonsberg yesterday, the 22d of August. It is only twelve or thirteen English miles to Moss, through a country, less wild than any tract I had hitherto passed over in Norway. It was often beautiful; but seldom afforded those grand views, which fill, rather than sooth the mind.

We glided along the meadows, and through the woods, with sun-beams playing around us; and though no castles adorned the prospects, a greater number of comfortable farms met my eyes, during this ride, than I have ever seen, in the same space, even in the most cultivated part of England. And the very appearance of the cottages of the labourers, sprinkled amidst them, excluded all those gloomy ideas inspired by the contemplation of poverty.

The hay was still bringing in; for one harvest in Norway, treads on the heels of the other. The woods were more variegated; interspersed with shrubs. We no longer passed through forests of vast pines, stretching along with savage magnificence. Forests that only exhibited the slow decay of time, or the devastation produced by warring elements. No; oaks, ashes, beech; and all the light and graceful tenants of our woods here sported luxuriantly. I had not observed many oaks before; for the greater part of the oak planks, I am informed, come from the westward.

In France the farmers generally live in villages, which is a great disadvantage to the country; but the Norwegian farmers, always owning their farms, or being tenants for life, reside in the midst of them; allowing some labourers a dwelling, rent free, who have a little land appertaining to the cottage, not only for a garden, but for crops of different kinds, such as rye, oats, buckwheat, hemp, flax, beans, potatoes, and hay, which are sown in strips about it; reminding a stranger of the first attempts at culture, when every family was obliged to be an independent community.

These cottagers work at a certain price, ten-pence per day, for the farmers on whose ground they live; and they have spare time enough to cultivate their own land; and lay in a store of fish for the winter. The wives and daughters spin; and the husbands and sons weave; so that they may fairly be reckoned independent; having also a little money in hand to buy coffee, brandy, and some other superfluities.

The only thing I disliked was the military service, which trammels them more than I at first imagined. It is true that the militia is only called out once a year— yet, in case of war, they have no alternative, but must abandon their families. Even the manufacturers are not exempted, though the miners are, in order to encourage undertakings which require a capital at the commencement. And what appears more tyrannical, the inhabitants of certain districts are appointed for the land, others for the sea service. Consequently, a peasant, born a soldier, is not permitted to follow his inclination, should it lead him to go to sea: a natural desire near so many sea ports.

In these regulations the arbitrary government, the king of Denmark being the most absolute monarch in Europe, appears, which in other respects, seeks to hide itself in a lenity that almost renders the laws nullities. If any alteration of old customs is thought of, the opinion of the whole country is required, and maturely considered. I have several times had occasion to observe, that fearing to appear tyrannical, laws are allowed to become obsolete, which ought to be put in force, or better substituted in their stead; for this mistaken moderation, which borders on timidity, favours the least respectable part of the people.

I saw on my way not only good parsonage houses, but comfortable dwellings, with glebe land[1] for the clerk: always a consequential man in every country: a being proud of a little smattering of learning, to use the appropriate epithet, and vain of the stiff good-breeding reflected from the vicar; though the servility practised in his company gives it a peculiar cast.

The widow of the clergyman is allowed to receive the benefit of the living for a twelve-month, after the death of the incumbent.

Arriving at the ferry, the passage over to Moss is about six or eight English miles; I saw the most level shore I had yet seen in Norway. The appearance of the circumjacent country had been preparing me for the change of scene, which was to greet me, when I reached the coast. For the grand features of nature had been

---

1. Church-owned land lent as part of a clergyman's benefice.

dwindling into prettiness as I advanced; yet the rocks, on a smaller scale, were finely wooded to the water's edge. Little art appeared, yet sublimity every where gave place to elegance. The road had often assumed the appearance of a graveled one, made in pleasure grounds, whilst the trees excited only an idea of embellishment. Meadows, like lawns, in an endless variety, displayed the careless graces of nature; and the ripening corn[2] gave a richness to the landscape, analogous with the other objects.

Never was a southern sky more beautiful, nor more soft its gales. Indeed, I am led to conclude, that the sweetest summer in the world, is the northern one. The vegetation being quick and luxuriant, the moment the earth is loosened from its icy fetters, and the bound streams regain their wonted activity. The balance of happiness, with respect to climate, may be more equal than I at first imagined; for the inhabitants described with warmth the pleasures of a winter, at the thoughts of which I shudder. Not only their parties of pleasure but of business are reserved for this season, when they travel with astonishing rapidity, the most direct way, skimming over hedge and ditch.

On entering Moss I was struck by the animation which seemed to result from industry. The richest of the inhabitants keep shops, resembling in their manners, and even the arrangement of their houses, the trades people of Yorkshire; with an air of more independence, or rather consequence, from feeling themselves the first people in the place. I had not time to see the iron works, belonging to Mr. Anker, of Christiania, a man of for-

---

2. The word is used in the usual English sense of a grain-producing crop, here probably wheat.

tune and enterprise; and I was not very anxious to see them, after having viewed those at Laurvig.

Here I met with an intelligent literary man, who was anxious to gather information from me, relative to the past and present situation of France. The newspapers printed at Copenhagen, as well as those in England, give the most exaggerated accounts of their atrocities and distresses; but the former without any apparent comments or inferences. Still the Norwegians, though more connected with the English, speaking their language, and copying their manners, wish well to the republican cause; and follow, with the most lively interest, the successes of the French arms. So determined were they, in fact, to excuse every thing, disgracing the struggle of freedom, by admitting the tyrant's plea necessity, that I could hardly persuade them that Robespierre was a monster.[3]

The discussion of this subject is not so general as in England, being confined to the few, the clergy and physician, with a small portion of people who have a literary turn and leisure: the greater part of the inhabitants, having a variety of occupations, being owners of ships, shopkeepers and farmers, have employment enough at home. And their ambition to become rich may tend to cultivate the common sense, which characterizes and narrows both their hearts and views; confining the former to their families, taking the *handmaids* of it into the circle of pleasure, if not of interest; and the latter to the inspection of their workmen, including the noble science of bargain-making—that is getting every thing at the cheapest, and selling it at the dearest rate.

---

3. The radical principles of this fanatical French leader of the Jacobins led to the Terror. He was himself executed in 1794.

LETTER XIII

I am now more than ever convinced, that it is an inter-course with men of science and artists, which not only diffuses taste, but gives that freedom to the under-standing, without which I have seldom met with much benevolence of character, on a large scale.

Besides, though you do not hear of much pilfering and stealing in Norway, yet they will, with a quiet conscience, buy things at a price which must convince them they were stolen. I had an opportunity of know-ing that two or three reputable people had purchased some articles of vagrants, who were detected. How much of the virtue, which appears in the world, is put on for the world! And how little dictated by self respect —so little, that I am ready to repeat the old question— and ask, where is truth or rather principle to be found? These are, perhaps, the vapourings of a heart ill at ease —the effusions of a sensibility wounded almost to mad-ness. But enough of this—we will discuss the subject in another state of existence—where truth and justice will reign. How cruel are the injuries which make us quarrel with human nature!—At present black melancholy hov-ers round my footsteps; and sorrow sheds a mildew over all the future prospects, which hope no longer gilds.

A rainy morning prevented my enjoying the pleasure the view of a picturesque country would have afforded me; for though this road passed through a country, a greater extent of which was under cultivation, than I had usually seen here, it nevertheless retained all the wild charms of Norway. Rocks still enclosed the val-leys, whose grey sides enlivened their verdure. Lakes appeared like branches of the sea, and branches of the sea assumed the appearance of tranquil lakes; whilst streamlets prattled amongst the pebbles, and the broken mass of stone which had rolled into them; giving fantastic turns to the trees whose roots they bared.

It is not, in fact, surprising that the pine should be often undermined, it shoots its fibres in such an horizontal direction, merely on the surface of the earth, requiring only enough to cover those that cling to the craggs. Nothing proves to me, so clearly, that it is the air which principally nourishes trees and plants, as the flourishing appearance of these pines.—The firs demanding a deeper soil, are seldom seen in equal health, or so numerous on the barren cliffs. They take shelter in the crevices, or where, after some revolving ages, the pines have prepared them a footing.

Approaching, or rather descending, to Christiania, though the weather continued a little cloudy, my eyes were charmed with the view of an extensive undulated valley, stretching out under the shelter of a noble amphitheatre of pine-covered mountains. Farm houses scattered about animated, nay, graced a scene which still retained so much of its native wildness, that the art which appeared, seemed so necessary it was scarcely perceived. Cattle were grazing in the shaven meadows; and the lively green, on their swelling sides, contrasted with the ripening corn and rye. The corn that grew on the slopes, had not, indeed, the laughing luxuriance of plenty, which I have seen in more genial climes. A fresh breeze swept across the grain, parting its slender stalks; but the wheat did not wave its head with its wonted, careless dignity, as if nature had crowned it the king of plants.

The view, immediately on the left, as we drove down the mountain, was almost spoilt by the depredations committed on the rocks to make alum. I do not know the process.—I only saw that the rocks looked red after they had been burnt; and regretted that the operation should leave a quantity of rubbish, to introduce an image of human industry in the shape of destruction.[4] The situation of Christiania is certainly uncommonly fine; and I never saw a bay that so forcibly gave me an idea of a place of safety from the storms of the ocean—all the surrounding objects were beautiful, and even grand. But neither the rocky mountains, nor the woods that graced them, could be compared with the sublime prospects I had seen towards the westward; and as for the hills, "capped with *eternal* snow," Mr. Coxe's[5] description led me to look for them; but they had flown; for I looked vainly around for this noble back-ground.

A few months ago the people of Christiania rose, exasperated by the scarcity, and consequent high price of grain. The immediate cause was the shipping of some, said to be for Moss; but which they suspected was only a pretext to send it out of the country: and I am not sure that they were wrong in their conjecture.— Such are the tricks of trade! They threw stones at Mr. Anker, the owner of it, as he rode out of town to escape from their fury; they assembled about his house. And the people demanded afterwards, with so much impetuosity, the liberty of those who were taken up in consequence of the tumult, that the Grand Bailiff thought it prudent to release them without further altercation.

You may think me too severe on commerce; but from the manner it is at present carried on, little can be advanced in favour of a pursuit that wears out the most

---

4. Alum was made at the time by roasting alunite with coal, exposing it to air, then extracting the crystals with hot water. The residue left behind contained iron salts, accounting for the red hue Wollstonecraft mentions.

5. John Lillard (pseud. Henry Coxe), author of a popular guide.

sacred principles of humanity and rectitude. What is speculation, but a species of gambling, I might have said fraud, in which address generally gains the prize? I was led into these reflections when I heard of some tricks practised by merchants, mis-called reputable, and certainly men of property, during the present war, in which common honesty was violated: damaged goods, and provisions, having been shipped for the express purpose of falling into the hands of the English, who had pledged themselves to reimburse neutral nations, for the cargoes they seized: cannon also, sent back as unfit for service, have been shipped as *a good speculation;* the captain receiving orders to cruize about till he fell in with an English frigate. Many individuals, I believe, have suffered by the seizures of their vessels; still I am persuaded that the English government has been very much imposed upon in the charges made by merchants, who contrived to get their ships taken. This censure is not confined to the Danes. Adieu! For the present, I must take advantage of a moment of fine weather to walk out and see the town.

At Christiania I met with that polite reception, which rather characterises the progress of manners in the world, than of any particular portion of it. The first evening of my arrival I supped with some of the most fashionable people of the place; and almost imagined myself in a circle of English ladies, so much did they resemble them in manners, dress, and even in beauty; for the fairest of my countrywomen would not have been sorry to rank with the Grand Bailiff's lady. There were several pretty girls present, but she outshone them all; and what interested me still more, I could not avoid observing that in acquiring the easy politeness which distinguishes people of quality, she had preserved her Norwegian simplicity. There was, in fact, a graceful timidity in her address, inexpressibly charming. This surprised me a little, because her husband was quite a Frenchman of the *ancien regime,* or rather a courtier, the same kind of animal in every country.

Here I saw the cloven foot of despotism. I boasted, to you, that they had no viceroy in Norway; but these grand bailiffs, particularly the superior one, who resides at Christiania, are political monsters of the same species. Needy sycophants are provided for by their relations and connexions at Copenhagen, as at other courts. And though the Norwegians are not in the abject state of the Irish, yet this second-hand government is still felt by their being deprived of several natural advantages to benefit the domineering state.[6]

The grand bailiffs are mostly noblemen from Copenhagen, who act as men of common minds will always act in such situations—aping a degree of courtly parade which clashes with the independent character of a magistrate. Besides, they have a degree of power over the country judges, which some of them who exercise a jurisdiction truly patriarchal, most painfully feel. I can scarcely say why, my friend, but in this city, thoughtfulness seemed to be sliding into melancholy, or rather dullness.—The fire of fancy, which had been kept alive in the country, was almost extinguished by reflections on the ills that harass such a large portion of mankind.

---

6. The rule of Ireland by absentee British landlords, the exploitation of their colony's products for England's gain, and the poverty of the mass of the people were shocking to many intelligent British in the eighteenth century, notably Jonathan Swift and, of course, Mary Wollstonecraft.

LETTER XIII

—I felt like a bird fluttering on the ground unable to mount; yet unwilling to crawl tranquilly like a reptile, whilst still conscious it had wings. I walked out, for the open air is always my remedy when an aching-head proceeds from an oppressed heart. Chance directed my steps towards the fortress, and the sight of the slaves, working with chains on their legs, only served to embitter me still more against the regulations of society, which treated knaves in such a different manner, especially as there was a degree of energy in some of their countenances which unavoidably excited my attention, and almost created respect.

I wished to have seen, through an iron grate, the face of a man who has been confined six years, for having induced the farmers to revolt against some impositions of the government. I could not obtain a clear account of the affair; yet, as the complaint was against some farmers of taxes, I am inclined to believe, that it was not totally without foundation. He must have possessed some eloquence, or have had truth on his side; for the farmers rose by hundreds to support him, and were very much exasperated at his imprisonment; which will probably last for life, though he has sent several very spirited remonstrances to the upper court, which makes the judges so averse to giving a sentence which may be cavilled at, that they take advantage of the glorious uncertainty of the law, to protract a decision which is only to be regulated by reasons of state.

The greater number of the slaves, I saw here, were not confined for life. Their labour is not hard; and they work in the open air, which prevents their constitutions from suffering by imprisonment. Still as they are allowed to associate together, and boast of their dexterity, not only to each other but to the soldiers around them,

LETTER XIII

in the garrison, they commonly, it is natural to conclude, go out more confirmed, and more expert knaves
than when they entered.

It is not necessary to trace the origin of the association of ideas, which led me to think that the stars and
gold keys, which surrounded me the evening before,
disgraced the wearers, as much as the fetters I was
viewing—perhaps more. I even began to investigate the
reason which led me to suspect that the former produced the latter.

The Norwegians are extravagantly fond of courtly
distinction, and of titles, though they have no immuni-
ties annexed to them, and are easily purchased. The
proprietors of mines have many privileges: they are
almost exempt from taxes, and the peasantry born on
their estates, as well as those on the count's, are not born
soldiers or sailors.

One distinction, or rather trophy of nobility, which
might have occurred to the Hottentots,[7] amused me; it
was a bunch of hog's bristles placed on the horses'
heads; surmounting that part of the harness to which a
round piece of brass often dangles, fatiguing the eye
with its idle motion.

From the fortress I returned to my lodging, and
quickly was taken out of town to be shewn a pretty
villa, and English garden. To a Norwegian both might
have been objects of curiosity, and of use, by exciting
to the comparison which leads to improvement. But
whilst I gazed, I was employed in restoring the place to

7. The term is evidently used here not specifically in reference to the
South African tribe, but to suggest an uncivilized person of inferior intellect.
Wollstonecraft was an egalitarian and deeply opposed to the slave trade, but
she had not progressed to what could be called complete humanitarianism.

nature, or taste, by giving it the character of the surrounding scene. Serpentine walks, and flowering shrubs, looked trifling in a grand recess of the rocks, shaded by towering pines. Groves of lesser trees might have been sheltered under them, which would have melted into the landscape, displaying only the art which ought to point out the vicinity of a human abode, furnished with some elegance. But few people have sufficient taste to discern, that the art of embellishing, consists in interesting, not in astonishing.

Christiania is certainly very pleasantly situated; and the environs I passed through, during this ride, afforded many fine, and cultivated prospects; but, excepting the first view approaching to it, rarely present any combination of objects so strikingly new, or picturesque, as to command remembrance.

Adieu!

LETTER XIV

CHRISTIANIA is a clean, neat city; but it has none of
the graces of architecture, which ought to keep pace
with the refining manners of a people—or the outside
of the house will disgrace the inside; giving the beholder an idea of overgrown wealth devoid of taste.
Large square wooden houses offend the eye, displaying
more than gothic barbarism.[1] Huge gothic piles, indeed,
exhibit a characteristic sublimity, and a wildness of
fancy peculiar to the period when they were erected;
but size, without grandeur or elegance, has an emphati-
cal stamp of meanness, of poverty of conception, which
only a commercial spirit could give.

The same thought has struck me, when I have entered the meeting-house of my respected friend, Dr.
Price.[2] I am surprised that the dissenters, who have not

---

1. "Gothic" here is pejorative, meaning uncouth and savage, as opposed
to civilized, forces. In the sense of "medieval" the word, however, came to
be used later in the century in association with the supernatural, sublime, or
romantic; Wollstonecraft refers to the latter meaning in the next sentence.

2. Dr. Richard Price (1723–91), a liberal political thinker and famous
Dissenting minister (one who did not conform to the established church),
was a neighbor and friend of Wollstonecraft when she had her school on
Newington Green from 1783 to 1785.

laid aside all the pomps and vanities of life, should imagine a noble pillar, or arch, unhallowed. Whilst men have senses, whatever sooths them lends wings to devotion; else why do the beauties of nature, where all that charm them are spread around with a lavish hand, force even the sorrowing heart to acknowledge that existence is a blessing; and this acknowledgement is the most sublime homage we can pay to the Deity.

The argument of convenience is absurd. Who would labour for wealth, if it were to procure nothing but conveniencies? If we wish to render mankind moral from principle, we must, I am persuaded, give a greater scope to the enjoyments of the senses, by blending taste with them. This has frequently occurred to me since I have been in the north, and observed that there sanguine characters always take refuge in drunkenness after the fire of youth is spent.

But I have flown from Norway, to go back to the wooden houses. Farms constructed with logs, and even little villages, here erected in the same simple manner, have appeared to me very picturesque. In the more remote parts I had been particularly pleased with many cottages situated close to a brook, or bordering on a lake, with the whole farm contiguous. As the family increases, a little more land is cultivated: thus the country is obviously enriched by population. Formerly the farmers might more justly have been termed woodcutters. But now they find it necessary to spare the woods a little; and this change will be universally beneficial; for whilst they lived entirely by selling the trees they felled, they did not pay sufficient attention to husbandry; consequently, advanced very slowly in agricultural knowledge. Necessity will in future more and more spur them on; for the ground, cleared of wood, must be cultivated, or the farm loses its value: there is no waiting for food till another generation of pines be grown to maturity.

The people of property are very careful of their timber; and, rambling through a forest near Tonsberg, belonging to the count, I have stopt to admire the appearance of some of the cottages inhabited by a woodman's family—a man employed to cut down the wood necessary for the household and the estate. A little lawn was cleared, on which several lofty trees were left which nature had grouped, whilst the encircling firs sported with wild grace. The dwelling was sheltered by the forest, noble pines spreading their branches over the roof; and before the door a cow, goat, nag, and children, seemed equally content with their lot; and if contentment be all we can attain, it is, perhaps, best secured by ignorance.

As I have been most delighted with the country parts of Norway, I was sorry to leave Christiania, without going further to the north, though the advancing season admonished me to depart, as well as the calls of business and affection.

June and July are the months to make a tour through Norway; for then the evenings and nights are the finest I have ever seen; but towards the middle, or latter end of August, the clouds begin to gather, and summer disappears almost before it has ripened the fruit of autumn—even, as it were, slips from your embraces, whilst the satisfied senses seem to rest in enjoyment.

You will ask, perhaps, why I wished to go further northward. Why? not only because the country, from all I can gather, is most romantic, abounding in forests and lakes, and the air pure, but I have heard much of the intelligence of the inhabitants, substantial farmers, who have none of that cunning to contaminate their simplicity, which displeased me so much in the conduct of the people on the sea coast. A man, who has been detected in any dishonest act, can no longer live among them. He is universally shunned, and shame becomes the severest punishment. Such a contempt have they, in fact, for every species of fraud, that they will not allow the people on the western coast to be their countrymen; so much do they despise the arts for which those traders who live on the rocks are notorious.

The description I received of them carried me back to the fables of the golden age:[3] independence and virtue; affluence without vice; cultivation of mind, without depravity of heart; with "ever smiling liberty;" the nymph of the mountain.[4] —I want faith! My imagination hurries me forward to seek an asylum in such a retreat from all the disappointments I am threatened with; but reason drags me back, whispering that the world is still the world, and man the same compound of weakness and folly, who must occasionally excite love and disgust, admiration and contempt. But this description, though it seems to have been sketched by a fairy pencil, was given me by a man of sound understanding, whose fancy seldom appears to run away with him.

A law in Norway, termed the *odels right*,[5] has lately been modified, and probably will be abolished as an impediment to commerce. The heir of an estate had the power of re-purchasing it at the original purchase

---

3. See Letter I, note 2, above.
4. Milton, "L'Allegro," lines 35-36: "And in thy right hand lead with thee,/ The mountain nymph, sweet Liberty."
5. Literally, the inheritance of estate land held in absolute ownership.

money, making allowance for such improvements as were absolutely necessary, during the space of twenty years. At present ten is the term allowed for after thought; and when the regulation was made, all the men of abilities were invited to give their opinion whether it were better to abrogate or modify it. It is certainly a convenient and safe way of mortgaging land; yet the most rational men, whom I conversed with on the subject, seemed convinced that the right was more injurious than beneficial to society; still if it contribute to keep the farms in the farmers own hands, I should be sorry to hear that it were abolished.

The aristocracy in Norway, if we keep clear of Christiania, is far from being formidable; and it will require a long time to enable the merchants to attain a sufficient monied interest to induce them to reinforce the upper class, at the expence of the yeomanry, with whom they are usually connected.

England and America owe their liberty to commerce, which created a new species of power to undermine the feudal system. But let them beware of the consequence; the tyranny of wealth is still more galling and debasing than that of rank.

Farewel! I must prepare for my departure.

LETTER XV

I LEFT Christiania yesterday. The weather was not very fine; and having been a little delayed on the road, I found that it was too late to go round, a couple of miles, to see the cascade near Fredericstadt, which I had determined to visit. Besides, as Fredericstadt is a fortress, it was necessary to arrive there before they shut the gate.

The road along the river is very romantic, though the views are not grand; and the riches of Norway, its timber, floats silently down the stream, often impeded in its course by islands and little cataracts, the offspring, as it were, of the great one I had frequently heard described.

I found an excellent inn at Fredericstadt, and was gratified by the kind attention of the hostess, who, perceiving that my clothes were wet, took great pains to procure me, as a stranger, every comfort for the night.

It had rained very hard; and we passed[1] the ferry in the dark, without getting out of our carriage, which I think wrong, as the horses are sometimes unruly. Fatigue and melancholy, however, had made me regard-

---

1. Used in the now obsolete sense of "crossed over on."

less whether I went down or across the stream; and I did not know that I was wet before the hostess remarked it. My imagination has never yet severed me from my griefs—and my mind has seldom been so free as to allow my body to be delicate.[2]

How I am altered by disappointment! —When going to Lisbon,[3] the elasticity of my mind was sufficient to ward off weariness, and my imagination still could dip her brush in the rainbow of fancy, and sketch futurity in glowing colours. Now—but let me talk of something else—will you go with me to the cascade?

The cross road to it was rugged and dreary; and though a considerable extent of land was cultivated on all sides, yet the rocks were entirely bare, which surprised me, as they were more on a level with the surface than any I had yet seen. On inquiry, however, I learnt that some years since a forest had been burnt. This appearance of desolation was beyond measure gloomy, inspiring emotions that sterility had never produced. Fires of this kind are occasioned by the wind suddenly rising when the farmers are burning roots of trees, stalks of beans, &c. with which they manure the ground. The devastation must, indeed, be terrible, when this, literally speaking, wild fire, runs along the forest, flying from top to top, and crackling amongst the branches. The soil, as well as the trees, is swept away by the destructive torrent; and the country, despoiled of beauty and riches, is left to mourn for ages.

Admiring, as I do, these noble forests, which seem to bid defiance to time, I looked with pain on the ridge of

---

2. "When the mind's free,/ The body's delicate." vid. *King Lear*. [Author's note.] *King Lear*, III.iv.11–12.

3. See Letter VI, note 7, and Letter VIII, note 4.

rocks that stretched far beyond my eye, formerly crowned with the most beautiful verdure.

I have often mentioned the grandeur, but I feel myself unequal to the task of conveying an idea of the beauty and elegance of the scene when the spiral tops of the pines are loaded with ripening seed, and the sun gives a glow to their light green tinge, which is changing into purple, one tree more or less advanced, contrasting with another. The profusion with which nature has decked them, with pendant honours, prevents all surprise at seeing, in every crevice, some sapling struggling for existence. Vast masses of stone are thus encircled; and roots, torn up by the storms, become a shelter for a young generation. The pine and fir woods, left entirely to nature, display an endless variety; and the paths in the wood are not entangled with fallen leaves, which are only interesting whilst they are fluttering between life and death. The grey cobweb-like appearance of the aged pines is a much finer image of decay; the fibres whitening as they lose their moisture, imprisoned life seems to be stealing away. I cannot tell why —but death, under every form, appears to me like something getting free—to expand in I know not what element; nay I feel that this conscious being must be as unfettered, have the wings of thought, before it can be happy.

Reaching the cascade, or rather cataract, the roaring of which had a long time announced its vicinity, my soul was hurried by the falls into a new train of reflections. The impetuous dashing of the rebounding torrent from the dark cavities which mocked the exploring eye, produced an equal activity in my mind: my thoughts darted from earth to heaven, and I asked myself why I was chained to life and its misery? Still the tumultuous emotions this sublime object excited, were pleasurable; and, viewing it, my soul rose, with renewed dignity, above its cares—grasping at immortality—it seemed as impossible to stop the current of my thoughts, as of the always varying, still the same, torrent before me—I stretched out my hand to eternity, bounding over the dark speck of life to come.

We turned with regret from the cascade. On a little hill, which commands the best view of it, several obelisks are erected to commemorate the visits of different kings. The appearance of the river above and below the falls is very picturesque, the ruggedness of the scenery disappearing as the torrent subsides into a peaceful stream. But I did not like to see a number of saw-mills crowded together close to the cataracts; they destroyed the harmony of the prospect.

The sight of a bridge erected across a deep valley, at a little distance, inspired very dissimilar sensations. It was most ingeniously supported by mast-like trunks, just stript of their branches; and logs, placed one across the other, produced an appearance equally light and firm, seeming almost to be built in the air when we were below it; the height taking from the magnitude of the supporting trees give them a slender, graceful look.

There are two noble estates in this neighbourhood, the proprietors of which seem to have caught more than their portion of the enterprising spirit that is gone abroad. Many agricultural experiments have been made; and the country appears better enclosed and cultivated; yet the cottages had not the comfortable aspect of those I had observed near Moss, and to the westward. Man is always debased by servitude, of any description; and here the peasantry are not entirely free.

Adieu!

I almost forgot to tell you, that I did not leave Norway without making some inquiries after the monsters said to have been seen in the northern sea; but though I conversed with several captains, I could not meet with one who had ever heard any traditional description of them, much less had any ocular demonstration of their existence. Till the fact be better ascertained, I should think the account of them ought to be torn out of our Geographical Grammars.[4]

---

4. Though the usage now rarely occurs, "grammar" in this sense is any book which presents a body of knowledge in a methodical form.

LETTER XVI

I SET out from Fredericstadt about three o'clock in the afternoon, and expected to reach Stromstad before the night closed in; but the wind dying away, the weather became so calm, that we scarcely made any perceptible advances toward the opposite coast, though the men were fatigued with rowing.

Getting amongst the rocks and islands as the moon rose, and the stars darted forward out of the clear expanse, I forgot that the night stole on, whilst indulging affectionate reveries, the poetical fictions of sensibility; I was not, therefore, aware of the length of time we had been toiling to reach Stromstad. And when I began to look around, I did not perceive any thing to indicate that we were in its neighbourhood. So far from it, that when I inquired of the pilot, who spoke a little English, I found that he was only accustomed to coast along the Norwegian shore; and had been, only once, across to Stromstad. But he had brought with him a fellow better acquainted, he assured me, with the rocks by which they were to steer our course; for we had not a compass on board; yet, as he was half a fool, I had little confidence in his skill. There was then great reason to fear that we had lost our way, and were straying amidst a labyrinth of rocks, without a clue.

This was something like an adventure; but not of the most agreeable cast; besides, I was impatient to arrive at Stromstad, to be able to send forward, that night, a boy to order horses on the road to be ready; for I was unwilling to remain there a day, without having any thing to detain me from my little girl; and from the letters which I was impatient to get from you.

I began to expostulate, and even to scold the pilot, for not having informed me of his ignorance, previous to my departure. This made him row with more force; and we turned round one rock only to see another, equally destitute of the tokens we were in search of to tell us where we were. Entering also into creek after creek, which promised to be the entrance of the bay we were seeking, we advanced merely to find ourselves running aground.

The solitariness of the scene, as we glided under the dark shadows of the rocks, pleased me for a while; but the fear of passing the whole night thus wandering to and fro, and losing the next day, roused me. I begged the pilot to return to one of the largest islands, at the side of which we had seen a boat moored. As we drew nearer, a light, through a window on the summit, became our beacon; but we were farther off than I supposed.

With some difficulty the pilot got on shore, not distinguishing the landing place; and I remained in the boat, knowing that all the relief we could expect, was a man to direct us. After waiting some time, for there is an insensibility in the very movements of these people,[1] that would weary more than ordinary patience, he brought with him a man, who, assisting them to row, we landed at Stromstad a little after one in the morning.

It was too late to send off a boy; but I did not go to bed before I had made the arrangements necessary to enable me to set out as early as possible.

The sun rose with splendor. My mind was too active to allow me to loiter long in bed, though the horses did not arrive till between seven and eight. However, as I wished to let the boy, who went forward to order the horses, get considerably the start of me, I bridled-in my impatience.

This precaution was unavailing, for after the three first posts, I had to wait two hours, whilst the people at the post-house went, fair and softly, to the farm, to bid them bring up the horses, which were carrying in the first-fruits of the harvest. I discovered here that these sluggish peasants had their share of cunning. Though they had made me pay for a horse, the boy had gone on foot, and only arrived half an hour before me. This disconcerted the whole arrangement of the day; and being detained again three hours, I reluctantly determined to sleep at Quistram, two posts short of Uddervalla, where I had hoped to have arrived that night.

But, when I reached Quistram, I found I could not approach the door of the inn, for men, horses, and carts, cows, and pigs huddled together. From the concourse of people, I had met on the road, I conjectured that there was a fair in the neighbourhood, this crowd convinced me that it was but too true. The boisterous

---

1. It is very possible that he staid to smoke a pipe, though I was waiting in the cold. [Author's note.]

merriment that almost every instant produced a quarrel or made me dread one, with the clouds of tobacco, and fumes of brandy, gave an infernal appearance to the scene. There was every thing to drive me back, nothing to excite sympathy in a rude tumult of the senses, which I foresaw would end in a gross debauch. What was to be done? No bed was to be had, or even a quiet corner to retire to for a moment—all was lost in noise, riot, and confusion.

After some debating they promised me horses, which were to go on to Uddervalla, two stages. I requested something to eat first, not having dined; and the hostess, whom I have mentioned to you before, as knowing how to take care of herself, brought me a plate of fish, for which she charged a rix dollar and a half. This was making hay whilst the sun shone. I was glad to get out of the up-roar, though not disposed to travel in an incommodious open carriage all night, had I thought that there was any chance of getting horses.

Quitting Quistram, I met a number of joyous groups, and though the evening was fresh, many were stretched on the grass like weary cattle; and drunken men had fallen by the road side. On a rock, under the shade of lofty trees, a large party of men and women had lighted a fire, cutting down fuel around to keep it alive all night. They were drinking, smoking, and laughing, with all their might and main. I felt for the trees whose torn branches strewed the ground. —Hapless nymphs! thy haunts I fear were polluted by many an unhallowed flame; the casual burst of the moment!

The horses went on very well; but when we drew near the post-house, the postilion stopt short, and neither threats, nor promises, could prevail on him to go forward. He even began to howl and weep, when I insisted on his keeping his word. Nothing, indeed, can equal the stupid obstinacy of some of these half alive beings, who seem to have been made by Prometheus, when the fire he stole from Heaven was so exhausted, that he could only spare a spark to give life, not animation, to the inert clay.

It was some time before we could rouse any body; and, as I expected, horses we were told could not be had in less than four or five hours. I again attempted to bribe the churlish brute, who brought us there; but I discovered, that in spite of the courteous hostess's promise, he had received orders not to go any farther.

As there was no remedy I entered, and was almost driven back by the stench—a softer phrase would not have conveyed an idea of the hot vapour that issued from an apartment, in which some eight or ten people were sleeping, not to reckon the cats and dogs stretched on the floor. Two or three of the men or women were lying on the benches, others on old chests; and one figure started half out of a trunk to look at me, whom I might have taken for a ghost, had the *chemise* been white, to contrast with the sallow visage. But the *costume* of apparitions not being preserved I passed, nothing dreading, excepting the effluvia, warily amongst the pots, pans, milk-pails, and washing-tubs. After scaling a ruinous staircase, I was shewn a bed-chamber. The bed did not invite me to enter; opening, therefore, the window, and taking some clean towels out of my night-sack, I spread them over the coverlid, on which tired nature found repose, in spite of the previous disgust.

With the grey of the morn the birds awoke me; and descending to enquire for the horses, I hastened through the apartment, I have already described, not wishing to associate the idea of a pigstye with that of a human dwelling.

I do not now wonder that the girls lose their fine complexions at such an early age, or that love here is merely an appetite, to fulfil the main design of nature, never enlivened by either affection or sentiment.

For a few posts we found the horses waiting; but afterwards I was retarded, as before, by the peasants, who, taking advantage of my ignorance of the language, made me pay for the fourth horse, that ought to have gone forward to have the others in readiness, though it had never been sent. I was particularly impatient at the last post, as I longed to assure myself that my child was well.

My impatience, however, did not prevent my enjoying the journey. I had six weeks before passed over the same ground, still it had sufficient novelty to attract my attention, and beguile, if not banish, the sorrow that had taken up its abode in my heart. How interesting are the varied beauties of nature; and what peculiar charms characterize each season! The purple hue which the heath now assumed, gave it a degree of richness, that almost exceeded the lustre of the young green of spring —and harmonized exquisitely with the rays of the ripening corn. The weather was uninterruptedly fine, and the people busy in the fields cutting down the corn, or binding up the sheaves, continually varied the prospect. The rocks, it is true, were unusually rugged and dreary, yet as the road runs for a considerable way by the side of a fine river, with extended pastures on the other side, the image of sterility was not the predominant object, though the cottages looked still more miserable, after having seen the Norwegian farms. The trees, likewise, appeared of the growth of yesterday, compared with those Nestors[2] of the forest I have frequently mentioned. The women and children were cutting off branches from the beech, birch, oak, &c, and leaving them to dry—This way of helping out their fodder, injures the trees. But the winters are so long, that the poor cannot afford to lay in a sufficient stock of hay. By such means they just keep life in the poor cows, for little milk can be expected when they are so miserably fed.

It was Saturday, and the evening was uncommonly serene. In the villages I every where saw preparations for Sunday; and I passed by a little car loaded with rye, that presented, for the pencil and heart, the sweetest picture of a harvest home I had ever beheld. A little girl was mounted a straddle on a shaggy horse, brandishing a stick over its head; the father was walking at the side of the car with a child in his arms, who must have come to meet him with tottering steps, the little creature was stretching out its arms to cling around his neck; and a boy, just above petticoats, was labouring hard, with a fork, behind, to keep the sheaves from falling.

My eyes followed them to the cottage, and an involuntary sigh whispered to my heart, that I envied the mother, much as I dislike cooking, who was preparing their pottage. I was returning to my babe, who may never experience a father's care or tenderness. The bosom that nurtured her, heaved with a pang at the thought which only an unhappy mother could feel.

Adieu!

---

2. In Homeric legend a wise old counsellor of the Greeks; hence, suggesting anyone aged and wise.

LETTER XVII

I WAS unwilling to leave Gothenburg, without visiting
Trolhaettae. I wished not only to see the cascade, but
to observe the progress of the stupendous attempt to
form a canal through the rocks, to the extent of an
English mile and a half.[1]

This work is carried on by a company who employ
daily nine hundred men; five years was the time mentioned in the proposals, addressed to the public, as necessary for the completion. A much more considerable
sum than the plan requires has been subscribed, for
which there is every reason to suppose the promoters
will receive ample interest.

The Danes survey the progress of this work with a
jealous eye, as it is principally undertaken to get clear
of the Sound duty.

Arrived at Trolhaettae, I must own that the first view
of the cascade disappointed me: and the sight of the
works, as they advanced, though a grand proof of human industry, was not calculated to warm the fancy. I,

1. The Trollhätte Kanal, completed in 1800, connects Lake Vänern with
Gothenburg and the North Sea by a system of locks.

however, wandered about; and at last coming to the conflux of the various cataracts, rushing from different falls, struggling with the huge masses of rock, and rebounding from the profound cavities, I immediately retracted, acknowledging that it was indeed a grand object. A little island stood in the midst, covered with firs, which, by dividing the torrent, rendered it more picturesque; one half appearing to issue from a dark cavern, that fancy might easily imagine a vast fountain, throwing up its waters from the very centre of the earth.

I gazed I know not how long, stunned with the noise; and growing giddy with only looking at the never-ceasing tumultuous motion, I listened, scarcely conscious where I was, when I observed a boy, half obscured by the sparkling foam, fishing under the impending rock on the other side. How he had descended I could not perceive; nothing like human footsteps appeared; and the horrific craggs seemed to bid defiance even to the goat's activity. It looked like an abode only fit for the eagle, though in its crevices some pines darted up their spiral heads; but they only grew near the cascade; every where else sterility itself reigned with dreary grandeur; for the huge grey massy rocks which probably had been torn asunder by some dreadful convulsion of nature, had not even their first covering of a little cleaving moss. There were so many appearances to excite the idea of chaos, that, instead of admiring the canal and the works, great as they are termed, and little as they appear, I could not help regretting that such a noble scene had not been left in all its solitary sublimity. Amidst the awful roaring of the impetuous torrents, the noise of human instruments, and the bustle of workmen, even the blowing up of the rocks, when grand masses trembled in the darkened air—only resembled the insignificant sport of children.

One fall of water, partly made by art, when they were attempting to construct sluices, had an uncommonly grand effect; the water precipitated itself with immense velocity down a perpendicular, at least fifty or sixty yards, into a gulph, so concealed by the foam as to give full play to the fancy: there was a continual uproar: I stood on a rock to observe it, a kind of bridge formed by nature, nearly on a level with the commencement of the fall. After musing by it a long time, I turned towards the other side, and saw a gentle stream stray calmly out. I should have concluded that it had no communication with the torrent, had I not seen a huge log, that fell headlong down the cascade, steal peacefully into the purling stream.

I retired from these wild scenes with regret to a miserable inn, and next morning returned to Gothenburg, to prepare for my journey to Copenhagen.

I was sorry to leave Gothenburg, without travelling further into Sweden; yet I imagine I should only have seen a romantic country thinly inhabited, and these inhabitants struggling with poverty. The Norwegian peasantry, mostly independent, have a rough kind of frankness in their manner; but the Swedish, rendered more abject by misery, have a degree of politeness in their address, which, though it may sometimes border on insincerity, is oftener the effect of a broken spirit, rather softened than degraded by wretchedness.

In Norway there are no notes in circulation of less value than a Swedish rixdollar. A small silver coin, commonly not worth more than a penny, and never more than twopence, serves for change: but in Sweden they have notes as low as sixpence. I never saw any silver pieces there; and could not without difficulty, and giving a premium, obtain the value of a rixdollar, in a large copper coin, to give away on the road to the poor who open the gates.

As another proof of the poverty of Sweden, I ought to mention that foreign merchants, who have acquired a fortune there, are obliged to deposit the sixth part when they leave the kingdom. This law, you may suppose, is frequently evaded.

In fact, the laws here, as well as in Norway, are so relaxed, that they rather favour than restrain knavery.

Whilst I was at Gothenburgh, a man who had been confined for breaking open his master's desk, and running away with five or six thousand rixdollars, was only sentenced to forty days confinement on bread and water; and this slight punishment his relations rendered nugatory by supplying him with more savoury food.

The Swedes are in general attached to their families; yet a divorce may be obtained by either party, on proving the infidelity of the other, or acknowledging it themselves. The women do not often recur to this equal privilege; for they either retaliate on their husbands, by following their own devices, or sink into the merest domestic drudges, worn down by tyranny to servile submission. Do not term me severe, if I add, that after youth is flown, the husband becomes a sot; and the wife amuses herself by scolding her servants. In fact, what is to be expected in any country where taste and cultivation of mind do not supply the place of youthful beauty and animal spirits? Affection requires a firmer foundation than sympathy; and few people have a principle of action sufficiently stable to produce rectitude of feeling; for, in spite of all the arguments I have heard to justify deviations from duty, I am persuaded that even the most spontaneous sensations are more under the direction of principle than weak people are willing to allow.

But adieu to moralizing. I have been writing these last sheets at an inn in Elsineur, where I am waiting for horses; and as they are not yet ready, I will give you a short account of my journey from Gothenburg; for I set out the morning after I returned from Trolhaetta.

The country, during the first day's journey, presented a most barren appearance; as rocky, yet not so picturesque as Norway, because on a diminutive scale. We stopt to sleep at a tolerable inn in Falckersberg, a decent little town.

The next day beeches and oaks began to grace the prospects, the sea every now and then appearing to give them dignity. I could not avoid observing also, that even in this part of Sweden, one of the most sterile, as I was informed, there was more ground under cultivation than in Norway. Plains of varied crops stretched out to a considerable extent, and sloped down to the shore, no longer terrific.[2] And, as far as I could judge, from glancing my eye over the country, as we drove along, agriculture was in a more advanced state; though, in the habitations, a greater appearance of poverty still remained. The cottages indeed often looked most uncomfortable, but never so miserable as those I had remarked on the road to Stromstad; and the towns were equal, if not superior to many of the little towns in Wales, or some I have passed through on my way from Calais to Paris.

---

2. Terrifying by reason of its jagged and precipitous nature.

The inns, as we advanced, were not to be complained of, unless I had always thought of England. The people were civil, and much more moderate in their demands than the Norwegians, particularly to the westward, where they boldly charge for what you never had, and seem to consider you, as they do a wreck, if not as lawful prey, yet as a lucky chance, which they ought not to neglect to seize.

The prospect of Elsineur, as we passed the Sound, was pleasant. I gave three rixdollars for my boat, including something to drink. I mention the sum, because they impose on strangers.

Adieu! till I arrive at Copenhagen.

LETTER XVIII

COPENHAGEN

THE DISTANCE from Elsineur to Copenhagen is twenty-two miles; the road is very good, over a flat country diversified with wood, mostly beech, and decent mansions. There appeared to be a great quantity of corn land; and the soil looked much more fertile than it is in general so near the sea. The rising grounds indeed were very few; and around Copenhagen it is a perfect plain, and of course has nothing to recommend it, but cultivation, not decorations. If I say that the houses did not disgust me, I tell you all I remember of them; for I cannot recollect any pleasurable sensations they excited; or that any object, produced by nature or art, took me out of myself. The view of the city, as we drew near, was rather grand, but, without any striking feature to interest the imagination, excepting the trees which shade the foot-paths.

Just before I reached Copenhagen, I saw a number of tents on a wide plain, and supposed that the rage for encampments[1] had reached this city; but I soon discovered that they were the asylum of many of the poor

---

1. "Encampments" is the eighteenth-century equivalent of "camping," or lodging in the open air in tents, for recreation.

families who had been driven out of their habitations by the late fire.[2]

Entering soon after, I passed amongst the dust and rubbish it had left, affrighted by viewing the extent of the devastation; for at least a quarter of the city had been destroyed. There was little in the appearance of fallen bricks and stacks of chimneys to allure the imagination into soothing melancholy reveries; nothing to attract the eye of taste, but much to afflict the benevolent heart. The depredations of time have always something in them to employ the fancy, or lead to musing on subjects which, withdrawing the mind from objects of sense, seem to give it new dignity: but here I was treading on live ashes. The sufferers were still under the pressure of the misery occasioned by this dreadful conflagration. I could not take refuge in the thought; *they suffered—but they are no more!* a reflection I frequently summon to calm my mind, when sympathy rises to anguish: I therefore desired the driver to hasten to the hotel recommended to me, that I might avert my eyes, and snap the train of thinking which had sent me into all the corners of the city, in search of houseless heads.

This morning I have been walking round the town, till I am weary of observing the ravages. I had often heard the Danes, even those who had seen Paris and London, speak of Copenhagen with rapture. Certainly I have seen it in a very disadvantageous light, some of the best streets having been burnt and the whole place thrown into confusion. Still the utmost that can, or could ever, I believe, have been said in its praise, might be comprised in a few words. The streets are open, and

---

2. The Copenhagen fire of 1795 had destroyed the Town Hall, the Church of St. Nicholas, and nearly a thousand homes.

many of the houses large; but I saw nothing to rouse the idea of elegance or grandeur, if I except the circus where the king and prince royal reside.

The palace, which was consumed about two years ago, must have been a handsome spacious building:[3] the stone-work is still standing; and a great number of the poor, during the late fire, took refuge in its ruins, till they could find some other abode. Beds were thrown on the landing places of the grand stair-case, where whole families crept from the cold, and every little nook is boarded up as a retreat for some poor creatures deprived of their home. At present a roof may be sufficient to shelter them from the night air; but as the season advances, the extent of the calamity will be more severely felt, I fear, though the exertions on the part of government are very considerable. Private charity has also, no doubt, done much to alleviate the misery which obtrudes itself at every turn; still public spirit appears to me to be hardly alive here. Had it existed, the conflagration might have been smothered in the beginning, as it was at last, by tearing down several houses before the flames had reached them. To this the inhabitants would not consent; and the prince royal[4] not having sufficient energy of character to know when he ought to be absolute, calmly let them pursue their own course, till the whole city seemed to be threatened with destruction. Adhering, with puerile scrupulosity, to the law,

3. The Royal Palace, built between 1731 and 1745 by Christian IV, had fallen in flames in 1794.

4. Crown Prince Frederik (the future King Frederik VI), son of Christian VII and Caroline Matilda (see note 6 below), had assumed the powers of the regency in 1784, and was the effective ruler until his father's death in 1808.

which he has imposed on himself, of acting exactly right, he did wrong by idly lamenting, whilst he marked the progress of a mischief that one decided step would have stopt. He was afterwards obliged to resort to violent measures; but then—who could blame him? And, to avoid censure, what sacrifices are not made by weak minds!

A gentleman, who was a witness of the scene, assured me, likewise, that if the people of property had taken half as much pains to extinguish the fire, as to preserve their valuables and furniture, it would soon have been got under. But they who were not immediately in danger did not exert themselves sufficiently, till fear, like an electrical shock, roused all the inhabitants to a sense of the general evil. Even the fire engines were out of order, though the burning of the palace ought to have admonished them of the necessity of keeping them in constant repair. But this kind of indolence, respecting what does not immediately concern them, seems to characterize the Danes. A sluggish concentration in themselves makes them so careful to preserve their property, that they will not venture on any enterprise to increase it, in which there is a shadow of hazard.

Considering Copenhagen as the capital of Denmark and Norway, I was surprised not to see so much industry or taste as in Christiania. Indeed from every thing I have had an opportunity of observing, the Danes are the people who have made the fewest sacrifices to the graces.

The men of business are domestic tyrants, coldly immersed in their own affairs, and so ignorant of the state of other countries, that they dogmatically assert that Denmark is the happiest country in the world; the prince royal the best of all possible princes; and count Bernstorff the wisest of ministers.[5]

As for the women, they are simply notable house-wives; without accomplishments, or any of the charms that adorn more advanced social life. This total igno-rance may enable them to save something in their kitch-ens; but it is far from rendering them better parents. On the contrary, the children are spoilt; as they usually are, when left to the care of weak, indulgent mothers, who having no principle of action to regulate their feelings, become the slaves of infants, enfeebling both body and mind by false tenderness.

I am perhaps a little prejudiced, as I write from the impression of the moment; for I have been tormented to-day by the presence of unruly children, and made angry by some invectives thrown out against the mater-nal character of the unfortunate Matilda.[6] She was cen-sured, with the most cruel insinuation, for her management of her son; though, from what I could gather, she gave proofs of good sense, as well as tender-

5. Andreas Peter Bernstorff, nephew of the Foreign Minister of Christian VII, was an able administrator who kept Denmark from being embroiled in troubles the country could not handle.

6. Caroline Matilda, sister of George III and a Hanover, had in 1766 been married by proxy at age fifteen to Christian VII, who, after his father drank himself to death, had succeeded to the throne in 1766 at the age of seventeen. Christian VII was himself depraved in mind and body, and his marriage, rather than reforming him as had been hoped, gave him a new object for his cruelty: his wife and queen. A gifted doctor from Altona named Struen-see came as court physician and soon had the king under his influence (probably by the use of cocaine) and seduced Matilda. A daughter, Louise, was born to Struensee and Matilda, and Christian VII was forced to claim her. A secret plot of the Crown Prince Frederik and the Queen Dowager Juliane Marie brought about the fall of Struensee, who was condemned to die a barbarous death, by beheading followed by being drawn and quartered. Matilda, who had been ordered imprisoned, was rescued by an English warship and taken to Celle in Hanover, where she died in 1775 at the age of twenty-four.

ness in her attention to him. She used to bathe him herself every morning; insisted on his being loosely clad; and would not permit his attendants to injure his digestion, by humouring his appetite. She was equally careful to prevent his acquiring haughty airs, and playing the tyrant in leading-strings. The queen dowager would not permit her to suckle him; but the next child being a daughter, and not the heir apparent of the crown, less opposition was made to her discharging the duty of a mother.

Poor Matilda! thou hast haunted me ever since my arrival; and the view I have had of the manners of the country, exciting my sympathy, has increased my respect for thy memory!

I am now fully convinced that she was the victim of the party she displaced, who would have overlooked, or encouraged, her attachment, had her lover not, aiming at being useful, attempted to overturn some established abuses before the people, ripe for the change, had sufficient spirit to support him when struggling in their behalf. Such indeed was the asperity sharpened against her, that I have heard her, even after so many years have elapsed, charged with licentiousness, not only for endeavouring to render the public amusements more elegant, but for her very charities, because she erected amongst other institutions, an hospital to receive foundlings. Disgusted with many customs which pass for virtues, though they are nothing more than observances of forms, often at the expence of truth, she probably ran into an error common to innovators, in wishing to do immediately what can only be done by time.

Many very cogent reasons have been urged by her friends to prove, that her affection for Struensee was never carried to the length alledged against her, by those who feared her influence. Be that as it may, she certainly was not a woman of gallantry; and if she had an attachment for him, it did not disgrace her heart or understanding, the king being a notorious debauchee, and an idiot into the bargain. As the king's conduct had always been directed by some favourite, they also endeavoured to govern him, from a principle of self-preservation, as well as a laudable ambition; but, not aware of the prejudices they had to encounter, the system they adopted displayed more benevolence of heart than soundness of judgement. As to the charge, still believed, of their giving the king drugs to injure his faculties, it is too absurd to be refuted. Their oppressors had better have accused them of dabbling in the black art; for the potent spell still keeps his wits in bondage.

I cannot describe to you the effect it had on me to see this puppet of a monarch moved by the strings which count Bernstorff holds fast; sit, with vacant eye, erect, receiving the homage of courtiers, who mock him with a shew of respect. He is, in fact, merely a machine of state, to subscribe the name of a king to the acts of the government, which, to avoid danger, have no value, unless countersigned by the prince royal; for he is allowed to be absolutely an idiot, excepting that now and then an observation, or trick, escapes him, which looks more like madness than imbecility.

What a farce is life! This effigy of majesty is allowed to burn down to the socket, whilst the hapless Matilda was hurried into an untimely grave.

> "As flies to wanton boys, are we to the gods;
> They kill us for their sport."7

Adieu!

---

7. *King Lear*, IV.i.36–37.

LETTER XIX

BUSINESS having obliged me to go a few miles out of town this morning, I was surprised at meeting a crowd of people of every description; and inquiring the cause, of a servant who spoke French, I was informed that a man had been executed two hours before, and the body afterwards burnt. I could not help looking with horror around—the fields lost their verdure—and I turned with disgust from the well-dressed women, who were returning with their children from this sight. What a spectacle for humanity! The seeing such a flock of idle gazers, plunged me into a train of reflections, on the pernicious effects produced by false notions of justice. And I am persuaded that till capital punishments be entirely abolished, executions ought to have every appearance of horrour given to them; instead of being, as they are now, a scene of amusement for the gaping crowd, where sympathy is quickly effaced by curiosity.

I have always been of opinion that the allowing actors to die, in the presence of the audience, has an immoral tendency; but trifling when compared with the ferocity acquired by viewing the reality as a show; for it seems to me, that in all countries the common people go to executions to see how the poor wretch plays his part, rather than to commiserate his fate, much less to think of the breach of morality which has brought him to such a deplorable end. Consequently executions, far from being useful examples to the survivors, have, I am persuaded, a quite contrary effect, by hardening the heart they ought to terrify. Besides, the fear of an ignominious death, I believe, never deterred any one from the commission of a crime; because, in committing it, the mind is roused to activity about present circumstances. It is a game at hazard, at which all expect the turn of the die in their own favour; never reflecting on the chance of ruin, till it comes. In fact, from what I saw, in the fortresses of Norway, I am more and more convinced that the same energy of character, which renders a man a daring villain, would have rendered him useful to society, had that society been well organized. When a strong mind is not disciplined by cultivation, it is a sense of injustice that renders it unjust.

Executions, however, occur very rarely at Copenhagen; for timidity, rather than clemency, palsies all the operations of the present government. The malefactor, who died this morning, would not, probably, have been punished with death at any other period; but an incendiary excites universal execration; and as the greater part of the inhabitants are still distressed by the late conflagration, an example was thought absolutely necessary; though, from what I can gather, the fire was accidental.

Not, but that I have very seriously been informed, that combustible materials were placed at proper distances, by the emissaries of Mr. Pitt;[1] and, to corrobo-

---

1. William Pitt was the prime minister of England in 1795.

rate the fact, many people insist, that the flames burst
out at once in different parts of the city; not allowing
the wind to have any hand in it. So much for the plot.
But the fabricators of plots in all countries build their
conjectures on the "baseless fabric of a vision";[2] and, it
seems even a sort of poetical justice, that whilst this
minister is crushing at home, plots of his own conjuring
up,[3] that on the continent, and in the north, he should,
with as little foundation, be accused of wishing to set
the world on fire.

I forgot to mention, to you, that I was informed, by
a man of veracity, that two persons came to the stake
to drink a glass of the criminal's blood, as an infallible
remedy for the apoplexy. And when I animadverted in
the company, where it was mentioned, on such a horri-
ble violation of nature, a Danish lady reproved me very
severely, asking how I knew that it was not a cure for
the disease? adding, that every attempt was justifiable in
search of health. I did not, you may imagine, enter into
an argument with a person the slave of such a gross
prejudice. And I allude to it not only as a trait of the
ignorance of the people, but to censure the government,
for not preventing scenes that throw an odium on the
human race.

Empiricism is not peculiar to Denmark; and I know
no way of rooting it out, though it be a remnant of
exploded witchcraft, till the acquiring a general knowledge of the component parts of the human frame,
become a part of public education.

---

2. *The Tempest,* IV.i.151: "And, like the baseless fabric of this vision. . . ."

3. England was at war with France, and Pitt was busy putting down what
he thought to be Jacobin plots in Great Britain.

Since the fire, the inhabitants have been very assidu-
ously employed in searching for property secreted during the confusion; and it is astonishing how many
people, formerly termed reputable, had availed themselves of the common calamity to purloin what the
flames spared. Others, expert at making a distinction
without a difference, concealed what they found, not
troubling themselves to enquire for the owners, though
they scrupled to search for plunder any where, but
amongst the ruins.

To be honester than the laws require, is by most
people thought a work of supererogation; and to slip
through the grate of the law, has ever exercised the
abilities of adventurers, who wish to get rich the short-
est way. Knavery, without personal danger, is an art,
brought to great perfection by the statesman and swin-
dler; and meaner knaves are not tardy in following their
footsteps.

It moves my gall to discover some of the commercial
frauds practised during the present war. In short, under
whatever point of view I consider society, it appears, to
me, that an adoration of property is the root of all evil.
Here it does not render the people enterprising, as in
America, but thrifty and cautious. I never, therefore,
was in a capital where there was so little appearance of
active industry; and as for gaiety, I looked in vain for
the sprightly gait of the Norwegians, who in every
respect appear to me to have got the start of them. This
difference I attribute to their having more liberty: a
liberty which they think their right by inheritance,
whilst the Danes, when they boast of their negative
happiness, always mention it as the boon of the prince
royal, under the superintending wisdom of count Bernstorff. Vassallage is nevertheless ceasing throughout the

kingdom, and with it will pass away that sordid avarice which every modification of slavery is calculated to produce.

If the chief use of property be power, in the shape of the respect it procures, is it not among the inconsistencies of human nature most incomprehensible, that men should find a pleasure in hoarding up property which they steal from their necessities, even when they are convinced that it would be dangerous to display such an enviable superiority? Is not this the situation of serfs in every country; yet a rapacity to accumulate money seems to become stronger in proportion as it is allowed to be useless.

Wealth does not appear to be sought for, amongst the Danes, to obtain the elegant luxuries of life; for a want of taste is very conspicuous at Copenhagen; so much so, that I am not surprised to hear that poor Matilda offended the rigid lutherans, by aiming to refine their pleasures. The elegance which she wished to introduce, was termed lasciviousness: yet I do not find that the absence of gallantry renders the wives more chaste, or the husbands more constant. Love here seems to corrupt the morals, without polishing the manners, by banishing confidence and truth, the charm as well as cement of domestic life. A gentleman, who has resided in this city some time, assures me that he could not find language to give me an idea of the gross debaucheries into which the lower order of people fall; and the promiscuous amours of the men of the middling class with their female servants, debases both beyond measure, weakening every species of family affection.

I have every where been struck by one characteristic difference in the conduct of the two sexes; women, in general, are seduced by their superiors, and men jilted by their inferiors; rank and manners awe the one, and cunning and wantonness subjugate the other; ambition creeping into the woman's passion, and tyranny giving force to the man's; for most men treat their mistresses as kings do their favourites: *ergo* is not man then the tyrant of the creation?

Still harping on the same subject, you will exclaim— How can I avoid it, when most of the struggles of an eventful life have been occasioned by the oppressed state of my sex: we reason deeply, when we forcibly feel.

But to return to the straight road of observation. The sensuality so prevalent appears to me to arise rather from indolence of mind, and dull senses, than from an exuberance of life, which often fructifies the whole character when the vivacity of youthful spirits begins to subside into strength of mind.

I have before mentioned that the men are domestic tyrants, considering them as fathers, brothers, or husbands; but there is a kind of interregnum between the reign of the father and husband, which is the only period of freedom and pleasure that the women enjoy. Young people, who are attached to each other, with the consent of their friends, exchange rings, and are permitted to enjoy a degree of liberty together, which I have never noticed in any other country. The days of courtship are therefore prolonged, till it be perfectly convenient to marry: the intimacy often becomes very tender: and if the lover obtain the privilege of a husband, it can only be termed half by stealth, because the family is wilfully blind. It happens very rarely that these honorary engagements are dissolved or disregarded, a stigma being attached to a breach of faith, which is thought more disgraceful, if not so criminal, as the violation of the marriage vow.

Do not forget that, in my general observations, I do not pretend to sketch a national character; but merely to note the present state of morals and manners, as I trace the progress of the world's improvement. Because, during my residence in different countries, my principal object has been to take such a dispassionate view of men as will lead me to form a just idea of the nature of man. And, to deal ingenuously with you, I believe I should have been less severe in the remarks I have made on the vanity and depravity of the French,[4] had I travelled towards the north before I visited France.

The interesting picture frequently drawn of the virtues of a rising people has, I fear, been fallacious, excepting the accounts of the enthusiasm which various public struggles have produced. We talk of the depravity of the French, and lay a stress on the old age of the nation; yet where has more virtuous enthusiasm been displayed than during the two last years, by the common people of France and in their armies? I am obliged sometimes to recollect the numberless instances which I have either witnessed, or heard well authenticated, to balance the account of horrours, alas! but too true. I am, therefore, inclined to believe that the gross vices which I have always seen allied with simplicity of manners, are the concomitants of ignorance.

What, for example, has piety, under the heathen or christian system, been, but a blind faith in things contrary to the principles of reason? And could poor rea-

---

4. See *Historical and Moral View of the French Revolution.* [Author's note.] Wollstonecraft is referring to her own work on the French Revolution published in 1794.

son make considerable advances, when it was reckoned the highest degree of virtue to do violence to its dictates? Lutherans preaching reformation, have built a reputation for sanctity on the same foundation as the catholics; yet I do not perceive that a regular attendance on public worship, and their other observances, make them a whit more true in their affections, or honest in their private transactions. It seems, indeed, quite as easy to prevaricate with religious injunctions as human laws, when the exercise of their reason does not lead people to acquire principles for themselves to be the criterion of all those they receive from others.

If travelling, as the completion of a liberal education, were to be adopted on rational grounds, the northern states ought to be visited before the more polished parts of Europe, to serve as the elements even of the knowledge of manners, only to be acquired by tracing the various shades in different countries. But, when visiting distant climes, a momentary social sympathy should not be allowed to influence the conclusions of the understanding; for hospitality too frequently leads travellers, especially those who travel in search of pleasure, to make a false estimate of the virtues of a nation; which, I am now convinced, bear an exact proportion to their scientific improvements.

Adieu.

LETTER XX

I HAVE formerly censured the French for their extreme attachment to theatrical exhibitions, because I thought that they tended to render them vain and unnatural characters. But I must acknowledge, especially as women of the town never appear in the Parisian, as at our theatres, that the little saving of the week is more usefully expended there, every Sunday, than in porter or brandy, to intoxicate or stupify the mind. The common people of France have a great superiority over that class in every other country on this very score. It is merely the sobriety of the Parisians which renders their fetes more interesting, their gaiety never becoming disgusting or dangerous; as is always the case when liquor circulates. Intoxication is the pleasure of savages, and of all those whose employments rather exhaust their animal spirits, than exercise their faculties. Is not this, in fact, the vice, both in England and the northern states of Europe, which appears to be the greatest impediment to general improvement? Drinking is here the principal relaxation of the men, including smoking; but the women are very abstemious, though they have no public amusements as a substitute. I ought to except one theatre,[1] which appears more than is necessary; for when I was there, it was not half full; and neither the ladies nor actresses displayed much fancy in their dress.

The play was founded on the story of the Mock Doctor;[2] and, from the gestures of the servants, who were the best actors, I should imagine contained some humour. The farce, termed ballat,[3] was a kind of pantomime, the childish incidents of which were sufficient to shew the state of the dramatic art in Denmark, and the gross taste of the audience. A magician, in the disguise of a tinker, enters a cottage where the women are all busy ironing, and rubs a dirty frying-pan against the linen. The women raise an hue-and-cry, and dance after him, rousing their husbands, who join in the dance, but get the start of them in the pursuit. The tinker, with the frying-pan for a shield, renders them immoveable, and blacks their cheeks. Each laughs at the other, unconscious of his own appearance; mean while the women enter to enjoy the sport, *"the rare fun,"* with other incidents of the same species.

The singing was much on a par with the dancing; the one as destitute of grace, as the other of expression; but the orchestra was well filled, the instrumental being far superior to the vocal music.

I have likewise visited the public library and museum, as well as the palace of Rosembourg.[4] This palace, now

---

1. The Royal Theatre, opened in 1748, was the theater's only home in Denmark until 1874.

2. Molière's *Le Médecin malgré lui*, first performed in 1666, was a farcical satire about a cunning woodcutter who pretends to be a doctor. Henry Fielding had based his *Mock Doctor* (1733) on it.

3. The Norwegian word *"ballade"* means both "ballad" (in the sense of music played for a dance) and "confusion" or "a row."

4. The Royal Library and the Royal Museum were established by Frederik III in the seventeenth century; Rosenborg Castle was built as Christian IV's "summer house" and became what it is now, a celebrated museum.

deserted, displays a gloomy kind of grandeur through-out; for the silence of spacious apartments always makes itself to be felt; I at least feel it; and I listen for the sound of my footsteps, as I have done at midnight to the ticking of the death-watch, encouraging a kind of fanci-ful superstition. Every object carried me back to past times, and impressed the manners of the age forcibly on my mind. In this point of view the preservation of old palaces, and their tarnished furniture, is useful; for they may be considered as historical documents.

The vacuum left by departed greatness was every where observable, whilst the battles and processions, pourtrayed on the walls, told you who had here excited revelry after retiring from slaughter; or dismissed pag-eantry in search of pleasure. It seemed a vast tomb, full of the shadowy phantoms of those who had played or toiled their hour out, and sunk behind the tapestry, which celebrated the conquests of love or war. Could they be no more—to whom my imagination thus gave life? Could the thoughts, of which there remained so many vestiges, have vanished quite away? And these beings, composed of such noble materials of thinking and feeling, have they only melted into the elements to keep in motion the grand mass of life? It cannot be! — As easily could I believe that the large silver lions, at the top of the banqueting room, thought and reasoned. But avaunt! ye waking dreams! —yet I cannot describe the curiosities to you.

There were cabinets full of baubles, and gems, and swords, which must have been wielded by giant's hand. The coronation ornaments wait quietly here till wanted; and the wardrobe exhibits the vestments which formerly graced these shews. It is a pity they do not lend them to the actors, instead of allowing them to perish ingloriously.

I have not visited any other palace, excepting Hirsholm; the gardens of which are laid out with taste, and command the finest views the country affords. As they are in the modern and English style, I thought I was following the footsteps of Matilda, who wished to multiply around her the images of her beloved country. I was also gratified by the sight of a Norwegian landscape in miniature, which with great propriety makes a part of the Danish king's garden. The cottage is well imitated, and the whole has a pleasing effect, particularly so to me who love Norway—it's peaceful farms and spacious wilds.

The public library consists of a collection much larger than I expected to see; and it is well arranged. Of the value of the Icelandic manuscripts[5] I could not form a judgment, though the alphabet of some of them amused me, by shewing what immense labour men will submit to, in order to transmit their ideas to posterity. I have sometimes thought it a great misfortune for individuals to acquire a certain delicacy of sentiment, which often makes them weary of the common occurrences of life; yet it is this very delicacy of feeling and thinking which probably has produced most of the performances that have benefited mankind. It might with propriety, perhaps, be termed the malady of genius; the cause of that characteristic melancholy which "grows with its growth, and strengthens with its strength."[6]

---

5. In the seventeenth century Árni Magnússon, an Icelander who was an official in the Danish government, oversaw the transferral of many of the Icelandic manuscripts to Copenhagen where they were housed in the Royal Library. The Arne-Magnean collection is priceless and our most important source of early Germanic myths.

6. Alexander Pope, *An Essay on Man*, II, 135–36: "The young disease [the principle of death], that must subdue at length,/Grows with his growth, and strengthens with his strength."

There are some good pictures in the royal museum
—Do not start—I am not going to trouble you with a
dull catalogue, or stupid criticisms on masters, to whom
time has assigned their just niche in the temple of fame;
had there been any by living artists of this country, I
should have noticed them, as making a part of the
sketches I am drawing of the present state of the place.
The good pictures were mixed indiscriminately with
the bad ones, in order to assort the frames. The same
fault is conspicuous in the new splendid gallery forming
at Paris;[7] though it seems an obvious thought that a
school for artists ought to be arranged in such a manner, as to shew the progressive discoveries and improvements in the art.

A collection of the dresses, arms, and implements of
the Laplanders attracted my attention, displaying that
first species of ingenuity which is rather a proof of
patient perseverance, than comprehension of mind. The
specimens of natural history, and curiosities of art, were
likewise huddled together without that scientific order
which alone renders them useful; but this may partly
have been occasioned by the hasty manner in which
they were removed from the palace, when in flames.

There are some respectable men of science here, but
few literary characters, and fewer artists. They want
encouragement, and will continue, I fear, from the
present appearance of things, to languish unnoticed a
long time; for neither the vanity of wealth, nor the

---

7. On 10 August 1793, the Grande Galerie of the Louvre was officially
opened; the building had been originally the king's palace. After years of
reconstruction, a Museum Commission during the Revolution set about col-
lecting, organizing, and displaying a wealth of art from royal collections as
well as many paintings confiscated from the estates of the escaping émigrés.

enterprising spirit of commerce, has yet thrown a glance that way.

Besides, the prince royal, determined to be œconomical, almost descends to parsimony; and perhaps depresses his subjects, by labouring not to oppress them; for his intentions always seem to be good—yet nothing can give a more forcible idea of the dullness which eats away all activity of mind, than the insipid routine of a court, without magnificence or elegance.

The prince, from what I can now collect, has very moderate abilities; yet is so well disposed, that count Bernstorff finds him as tractable as he could wish; for I consider the count as the real sovereign, scarcely behind the curtain; the prince having none of that obstinate self-sufficiency of youth, so often the fore-runner of decision of character. He, and the princess his wife, dine every day with the king, to save the expence of two tables. What a mummery it must be to treat as a king a being who has lost the majesty of man! But even count Bernstorff's morality submits to this standing imposition; and he avails himself of it sometimes, to soften a refusal of his own, by saying it is the *will* of the king, my master, when every body knows that he has neither will nor memory. Much the same use is made of him as, I have observed, some termagant wives make of their husbands; they would dwell on the necessity of obeying their husbands, poor passive souls, who never were allowed *to will*, when they wanted to conceal their own tyranny.

A story is told here of the king's formerly making a dog counsellor of state, because when the dog, accustomed to eat at the royal table, snatched a piece of meat off an old officer's plate, he reproved him jocosely, saying that he, *monsieur le chien*, had not the privilege of dining with his majesty; a privilege annexed to this distinction.

The burning of the palace was, in fact, a fortunate circumstance, as it afforded a pretext for reducing the establishment of the houshold, which was far too great for the revenue of the crown. The Prince Royal, at present, runs into the opposite extreme; and the formality, if not the parsimony, of the court, seems to extend to all the other branches of society, which I had an opportunity of observing; though hospitality still characterizes their intercourse with strangers.

But let me now stop; I may be a little partial, and view every thing with the jaundiced eye of melancholy —for I am sad—and have cause.

God bless you!

Branston & Wright

LETTER XXI

I HAVE seen count Bernstorff; and his conversation confirms me in the opinion I had previously formed of him;—I mean, since my arrival at Copenhagen. He is a worthy man, a little vain of his virtue *à la Necker*;[1] and more anxious not to do wrong, that is to avoid blame, than desirous of doing good; especially if any particular good demands a change. Prudence, in short, seems to be the basis of his character; and, from the tenour of the government, I should think inclining to that cautious circumspection which treads on the heels of timidity. He has considerable information, and some finesse; or he could not be a minister. Determined not to risk his popularity, for he is tenderly careful of his reputation, he will never gloriously fail like Struensee,[2] or disturb,

---

1. Jacques Necker, the Finance Minister of France, dismissed in 1781, recalled in 1788 by the Estates General, out of the belief that he was the only one who knew how to stop the deficit in the French treasury. His second dismissal, on 11 July 1789, angered the masses, who attacked the Bastille on 14 July. The King again recalled him, but Necker soon proved unequal to the admittedly difficult task of putting France's financial house in order, and he retired in 1790 to the care of his daughter, the celebrated Madame de Staël.

2. See Letter XVIII, note 5.

with the energy of genius, the stagnant state of the public mind.

I suppose that Lavater,[3] whom he invited to visit him two years ago, some say to fix the principles of the christian religion firmly in the prince royal's mind, found lines in his face to prove him a statesman of the first order; because he has a knack at seeing a great character in the countenances of men in exalted stations, who have noticed him, or his works. Besides, the count's sentiments relative to the French revolution, agreeing with Lavater's, must have ensured his applause.

The Danes, in general, seem extremely averse to innovation, and, if happiness only consist in opinion, they are the happiest people in the world; for I never saw any so well satisfied with their own situation. Yet the climate appears to be very disagreeable; the weather being dry and sultry, or moist and cold; the atmosphere never having that sharp, bracing purity, which in Norway prepares you to brave its rigours. I do not then hear the inhabitants of this place talk with delight of the winter, which is the constant theme of the Norwegians, on the contrary they seem to dread its comfortless inclemency.

The ramparts are pleasant, and must have been much more so before the fire, the walkers not being annoyed by the clouds of dust, which, at present, the slightest wind wafts from the ruins. The wind-mills, and the comfortable houses contiguous, belonging to the millers, as well as the appearance of the spacious barracks

3. Johann Kasper Lavater (1741–1801), the Swiss founder of the "science" of physiognomy, was a convinced and orthodox Christian who brought mysticism and mesmerism to bear upon his desire to find the divine elements in the human frame.

for the soldiers and sailors, tend to render this walk more agreeable. The view of the country has not much to recommend it to notice, but its extent and cultivation: yet as the eye always delights to dwell on verdant plains, especially when we are resident in a great city, these shady walks should be reckoned amongst the advantages procured by the government for the inhabitants. I like them better than the royal gardens, also open to the public, because the latter seem sunk in the heart of the city, to concentrate its fogs.

The canals, which intersect the streets, are equally convenient and wholesome; but the view of the sea, commanded by the town, had little to interest me whilst the remembrance of the various bold and picturesque shores, I had seen, was fresh in my memory. Still the opulent inhabitants, who seldom go abroad, must find the spots where they fix their country seats much pleasanter on account of the vicinity of the ocean.

One of the best streets in Copenhagen is almost filled with hospitals, erected by the government; and, I am assured, as well regulated as institutions of this kind are in any country; but whether hospitals, or workhouses, are any where superintended with sufficient humanity, I have frequently had reason to doubt.

The autumn is so uncommonly fine, that I am unwilling to put off my journey to Hamburg much longer, lest the weather should alter suddenly, and the chilly harbingers of winter catch me here, where I have nothing now to detain me but the hospitality of the families to whom I had recommendatory letters. I lodged at an hotel situated in a large open square, where the troops exercise, and the market is kept. My apartments were very good; and, on account of the fire, I was told that I should be charged very high; yet, paying my bill just now, I find the demands much lower in proportion than in Norway, though my dinners were in every respect better.

I have remained more at home, since I arrived at Copenhagen, than I ought to have done in a strange place; but the mind is not always equally active in search of information; and my oppressed heart too often sighs out,

> "How dull, flat, and unprofitable
> Are to me all the usages of this world—
> That it should come to this!"—4

Farewell! Fare thee well, I say—if thou can'st, repeat the adieu in a different tone.

---

4. *Hamlet*, I.ii.133–37. The first two lines should read: "How weary, stale, flat, and unprofitable/ Seem to me all the uses of this world. ..."

LETTER XXII

I ARRIVED at Corsoer the night after I quitted Copenhagen, purposing to take my passage across the Great Belt the next morning, though the weather was rather boisterous. It is about four and twenty miles; but as neither I nor my little girl are ever attacked by sea sickness, though who can avoid *ennui?* I enter a boat with the same indifference as I change horses; and as for danger, come when it may, I dread it not sufficiently to have any anticipating fears.

The road from Copenhagen was very good, through an open, flat country, that had little to recommend it to notice excepting the cultivation, which gratified my heart more than my eye.

I took a barge with a German baron, who was hastening back from a tour into Denmark, alarmed by the intelligence of the French having passed the Rhine. His conversation beguiled the time, and gave a sort of stimulus to my spirits, which had been growing more and more languid ever since my return to Gothenburg —you know why. I had often endeavoured to rouse myself to observation by reflecting that I was passing through scenes which I should probably never see again, and consequently ought not to omit observing; still I fell into reveries, thinking, by way of excuse, that enlargement of mind and refined feelings are of little use, but to barb the arrows of sorrow which waylay us every where, eluding the sagacity of wisdom, and rendering principles unavailing, if considered as a breastwork to secure our own hearts.

Though we had not a direct wind, we were not detained more than three hours and a half on the water, just long enough to give us an appetite for our dinner.

We travelled the remainder of the day, and the following night, in company with the same party, the German gentleman whom I have mentioned, his friend, and servant: the meetings, at the post-houses, were pleasant to me, who usually heard nothing but strange tongues around me. Marguerite and the child often fell asleep; and when they were awake, I might still reckon myself alone, as our train of thoughts had nothing in common. Marguerite, it is true, was much amused by the *costume* of the women; particularly by the *panier*[1] which adorned both their heads and tails: and, with great glee, recounted to me the stories she had treasured up for her family, when once more within the barriers of dear Paris; not forgetting, with that arch, agreeable vanity peculiar to the French, which they exhibit whilst half ridiculing it, to remind me of the importance she should assume when she informed her friends of all her journeys by sea and land—shewing the pieces of money she had collected, and stammering out a few foreign phrases, which she repeated in a true Parisian accent.

---

1. This word in French means both basket and hoop. [Author's note.]

Happy thoughtlessness; aye, and enviable harmless vanity, which thus produced a *gaité du coeur* worth all my philosophy.

The man I had hired at Copenhagen advised me to go round, about twenty miles, to avoid passing the Little Belt, excepting by a ferry, as the wind was contrary. But the gentlemen over-ruled his arguments, which we were all very sorry for afterwards when we found ourselves becalmed on the Little Belt ten hours, tacking about, without ceasing, to gain on the shore.

An over-sight likewise made the passage appear much more tedious, nay almost insupportable. When I went on board at the Great Belt, I had provided refreshments in case of detention, which remaining untouched, I thought not then any such precaution necessary for the second passage, misled by the epithet of little, though I have since been informed that it is frequently the longest. This mistake occasioned much vexation; for the child, at last, began to cry so bitterly for bread, that fancy conjured up before me the wretched Ugolino,[2] with his famished children; and I, literally speaking, enveloped myself in sympathetic horrours, augmented by every tear my babe shed; from which I could not escape, till we landed, and a luncheon of bread, and bason of milk, routed the spectres of fancy.

I then supped with my companions, with whom I was soon after to part for ever—always a most melancholy, death-like idea—a sort of separation of soul; for all the regret which follows those from whom fate separates us, seems to be something torn from ourselves.

---

2. The thirteenth-century Guelph leader who twice conquered Pisa; when captured, he and two of his sons and two grandsons were locked into a tower and starved to death. See Dante's *Inferno*, Canto XXXIII.

These were strangers I remember; yet when there is any
originality in a countenance, it takes its place in our
memory; and we are sorry to lose an acquaintance the
moment he begins to interest us, though picked up on
the highway. There was, in fact, a degree of intelligence, and still more sensibility in the features and conversation of one of the gentlemen, that made me regret
the loss of his society during the rest of the journey; for
he was compelled to travel post, by his desire to reach
his estate before the arrival of the French.

This was a comfortable inn, as were several others I
stopt at; but the heavy sandy roads were very fatiguing,
after the fine ones we had lately skimmed over both in
Sweden and Denmark. The country resembled the most
open part of England; laid out for corn, rather than
grazing: it was pleasant; yet there was little in the prospects to awaken curiosity, by displaying the peculiar
characteristics of a new country, which had so frequently stole me from myself in Norway. We often
passed over large uninclosed tracts, not graced with
trees, or at least very sparingly enlivened by them; and
the half-formed roads seemed to demand the landmarks,
set up in the waste, to prevent the traveller from straying far out of his way, and plodding through the wearisome sand.

The heaths were dreary, and had none of the wild
charms of those of Sweden and Norway to cheat time;
neither the terrific rocks, nor smiling herbage, grateful
to the sight, and scented from afar, made us forget their
length; still the country appeared much more populous;
and the towns, if not the farm-houses, were superiour
to those of Norway. I even thought that the inhabitants
of the former had more intelligence, at least I am sure
they had more vivacity in their countenances than I had

seen during my northern tour: their senses seemed awake to business and pleasure. I was, therefore, gratified by hearing once more the busy hum of industrious men in the day, and the exhilarating sounds of joy in the evening; for as the weather was still fine, the women and children were amusing themselves at their doors, or walking under the trees, which in many places were planted in the streets; and as most of the towns of any note were situated on little bays, or branches, of the Baltic, their appearance, as we approached, was often very picturesque, and, when we entered, displayed the comfort and cleanliness of easy, if not the elegance of opulent, circumstances. But the chearfulness of the people in the streets was particularly grateful to me, after having been depressed by the deathlike silence of those of Denmark, where every house made me think of a tomb. The dress of the peasantry is suited to the climate; in short, none of that poverty and dirt appeared, at the sight of which the heart sickens.

As I only stopt to change horses, take refreshment, and sleep, I had not an opportunity of knowing more of the country than conclusions, which the information gathered by my eyes enabled me to draw; and that was sufficient to convince me that I should much rather have lived in some of the towns I now pass through, than in any I had seen in Sweden or Denmark. The people struck me, as having arrived at that period when the faculties will unfold themselves; in short, they look alive to improvement, neither congealed by indolence, nor bent down by wretchedness to servility.

From the previous impression, I scarcely can trace from whence I received it, I was agreeably surprised to perceive such an appearance of comfort in this part of

Germany.[3] I had formed a conception of the tyranny of the petty potentates that had thrown a gloomy veil over the face of the whole country, in my imagination, that cleared away like the darkness of night before the sun. As I saw the reality, I should probably have discovered much lurking misery, the consequence of ignorant oppression, no doubt, had I had time to inquire into particulars; but it did not stalk abroad, and infect the surface over which my eye glanced. Yes, I am persuaded that a considerable degree of general knowledge pervades this country; for it is only from the exercise of the mind that the body acquires the activity from which I drew these inferences. Indeed the king of Denmark's German dominions, Holstein, appeared to me far superiour to any other part of his kingdom which had fallen under my view; and the robust rustics to have their muscles braced, instead of the *as it were* lounge of the Danish peasantry.

Arriving at Sleswick, the residence of prince Charles of Hesse-Cassel, the sight of the soldiers recalled all the unpleasing ideas of German despotism, which imperceptibly vanished as I advanced into the country. I viewed, with a mixture of pity and horrour, these beings training to be sold to slaughter, or be slaughtered, and fell into reflections, on an old opinion of mine, that it is the preservation of the species, not of individuals, which appears to be the design of the Deity throughout the whole of nature. Blossoms come forth only to be blighted; fish lay their spawn where it will be devoured: and what a large portion of the human race are born merely to be swept prematurely away. Does not this

---

3. The German duchies of Holstein and Schleswig were at this time under Danish rule by virtue of the treaty of Copenhagen (1767).

waste of budding life emphatically assert, that it is not men, but man, whose preservation is so necessary to the completion of the grand plan of the universe? Children peep into existence, suffer, and die; men play like moths about a candle, and sink into the flame: war, and "the thousand ills which flesh is heir to,"[4] mow them down in shoals, whilst the more cruel prejudices of society palsies existence, introducing not less sure, though slower decay.

The castle was heavy and gloomy; yet the grounds about it were laid out with some taste; a walk, winding under the shade of lofty trees, led to a regularly built, and animated town.

I crossed the draw-bridge, and entered to see this shell of a court in miniature, mounting ponderous stairs, it would be a solecism to say a flight, up which a regiment of men might have marched, shouldering their firelocks, to exercise in vast galleries, where all the generations of the princes of Hesse-Cassel might have been mustered rank and file, though not the phantoms of all the wretched they had bartered to support their state, unless these airy substances could shrink and expand, like Milton's devils, to suit the occasion.[5]

The sight of the presence-chamber, and of the canopy to shade the *fauteuil*,[6] which aped a throne, made me smile. All the world is a stage, thought I; and few are there in it who do not play the part they have learnt by rote; and those who do not, seem marks set up

---

4. *Hamlet*, III.i.62–63: "the thousand natural shocks/ That flesh is heir to."

5. See *Paradise Lost*, I.423–30, where devils can, Milton says, assume either sex and any shape, and, "Dilated or condensed, bright or obscure,/ Can execute their aery purposes."

6. French for "armchair."

to be pelted at by fortune; or rather as sign-posts, which point out the road to others, whilst forced to stand still themselves amidst the mud and dust.

Waiting for our horses, we were amused by observing the dress of the women, which was very grotesque and unwieldy. The false notion of beauty which prevails here, as well as in Denmark, I should think very inconvenient in summer, as it consists in giving a rotundity to a certain part of the body, not the most slim, when nature has done her part. This Dutch prejudice often leads them to toil under the weight of some ten or a dozen petticoats, which, with an enormous basket, literally speaking, as a bonnet, or a straw hat of dimensions equally gigantic, almost completely concealing the human form, as well as face divine,[7] often worth shewing—still they looked clean, and tript along, as it were, before the wind, with a weight of tackle that I could scarcely have lifted. Many of the country girls, I met, appeared to me pretty, that is, to have fine complexions, sparkling eyes, and a kind of arch, hoyden playfulness which distinguishes the village coquette. The swains, in their Sunday trim, attended some of these fair ones, in a more slouching pace, though their dress was not so cumbersome. The women seem to take the lead in polishing the manners every where, that being the only way to better their condition.

From what I have seen throughout my journey, I do not think the situation of the poor in England is much, if at all superiour to that of the same class in different parts of the world; and in Ireland, I am sure, it is much inferiour. I allude to the former state of England; for at present the accumulation of national wealth only in-

---

7. Probably an echo of William Blake; see Letter IV, note 4.

creases the cares of the poor, and hardens the hearts of the rich, in spite of the highly extolled rage for alms-giving.

You know that I have always been an enemy to what is termed charity, because timid bigots endeavouring thus to cover their *sins*, do violence to justice, till, acting the demi-god, they forget that they are men. And there are others who do not even think of laying up a treasure in heaven, whose benevolence is merely tyranny in disguise: they assist the most worthless, because the most servile, and term them helpless only in proportion to their fawning.

After leaving Sleswick, we passed through several pretty towns; Itzehol particularly pleased me: and the country still wearing the same aspect, was improved by the appearance of more trees and enclosures. But what gratified me most, was the population. I was weary of travelling four or five hours, never meeting a carriage, and scarcely a peasant—and then to stop at such wretched huts, as I had seen in Sweden, was surely sufficient to chill any heart, awake to sympathy, and throw a gloom over my favourite subject of contemplation, the future improvement of the world.

The farm-houses, likewise, with the huge stables, into which we drove, whilst the horses were putting to, or baiting, were very clean and commodious. The rooms, with a door into this hall-like stable and storehouse in one, were decent; and there was a compactness in the appearance of the whole family lying thus snugly together under the same roof, that carried my fancy back to the primitive times, which probably never existed with such a golden lustre as the animated imagination lends, when only able to seize the prominent features.

At one of them, a pretty young woman, with languishing eyes, of celestial blue, conducted us into a very neat parlour; and observing how loosely, and lightly, my little girl was clad, began to pity her in the sweetest accents, regardless of the rosy down of health on her cheeks. This same damsel was dressed, it was Sunday, with taste, and even coquetry, in a cotton jacket, ornamented with knots of blue ribbon, fancifully disposed to give life to her fine complexion. I loitered a little to admire her, for every gesture was graceful; and, amidst the other villagers, she looked like a garden lily suddenly rearing its head amongst grain, and corn-flowers. As the house was small, I gave her a piece of money, rather larger than it was my custom to give to the female waiters; for I could not prevail on her to sit down; which she received with a smile; yet took care to give it, in my presence, to a girl, who had brought the child a slice of bread; by which I perceived that she was the mistress, or daughter, of the house—and without doubt the *belle* of the village. There was, in short, an appearance of chearful industry, and of that degree of comfort which shut out misery, in all the little hamlets as I approached Hamburg, which agreeably surprised me.

The short jackets which the women wear here, as well as in France, are not only more becoming to the person, but much better calculated for women who have rustic or houshold employments, than the long gowns worn in England, dangling in the dirt.

All the inns on the road were better than I expected, though the softness of the beds still harassed me, and prevented my finding the rest I was frequently in want of, to enable me to bear the fatigue of the next day. The charges were moderate, and the people very civil, with a certain honest hilarity and independent spirit in their manner, which almost made me forget that they were inn-keepers, a set of men, waiters, hostesses, chambermaids, &c. down to the ostler, whose cunning servility, in England, I think particularly disgusting.

The prospect of Hamburg, at a distance, as well as the fine road shaded with trees, led me to expect to see a much pleasanter city than I found.

I was aware of the difficulty of obtaining lodgings, even at the inns, on account of the concourse of strangers at present resorting to such a centrical situation, and determined to go to Altona the next day to seek for an abode, wanting now only rest. But even for a single night we were sent from house to house, and found at last a vacant room to sleep in, which I should have turned from with disgust, had there been a choice.

I scarcely know any thing that produces more disagreeable sensations, I mean to speak of the passing cares, the recollection of which afterwards enlivens our enjoyments, than those excited by little disasters of this kind. After a long journey, with our eyes directed to some particular spot, to arrive and find nothing as it should be, is vexatious, and sinks the agitated spirits. But I, who received the cruelest of disappointments, last spring, in returning to my home, term such as these emphatically passing cares. Know you of what materials some hearts are made? I play the child, and weep at the recollection—for the grief is still fresh that stunned as well as wounded me—yet never did drops of anguish like these bedew the cheeks of infantine innocence— and why should they mine, that never were stained by a blush of guilt?[8] Innocent and credulous as a child, why have I not the same happy thoughtlessness?

Adieu!

---

8. Very likely Wollstonecraft is referring to her discovery that Gilbert Imlay had taken a mistress; these lines suggest she knew about it soon after her return to England from Paris in the spring of 1795.

LETTER XXIII

I MIGHT have spared myself the disagreeable feelings I experienced the first night of my arrival at Hamburg, leaving the open air to be shut up in noise and dirt, had I gone immediately to Altona, where a lodging had been prepared for me by a gentleman from whom I received many civilities during my journey. I wished to have travelled in company with him from Copenhagen, because I found him intelligent and friendly; but business obliged him to hurry forward; and I wrote to him on the subject of accommodations, as soon as I was informed of the difficulties I might have to encounter to house myself and brat.[1]

It is but a short and pleasant walk from Hamburg to Altona, under the shade of several rows of trees; and this walk is the more agreeable, after quitting the rough pavement of either place.

Hamburg is an ill, close-built town, swarming with inhabitants; and, from what I could learn, like all the other free towns, governed in a manner which bears

---

1. Because Wollstonecraft's tenderness for her child is so obvious, it seems likely that she is using "brat" without the perjorative overtones the word usually carries.

hard on the poor, whilst narrowing the minds of the rich, the character of the man is lost in the Hamburger. Always afraid of the encroachments of their Danish neighbours, that is, anxiously apprehensive of their sharing the golden harvest of commerce with them, or taking a little of the trade off their hands, though they have more than they know what to do with, they are ever on the watch, till their very eyes lose all expression, excepting the prying glance of suspicion.

The gates of Hamburg are shut at seven, in the winter, and nine in the summer, lest some strangers, who come to traffic in Hamburg, should prefer living, and consequently, so exactly do they calculate, spend their money out of the walls of the Hamburger's world. Immense fortunes have been acquired by the *per cents* arising from commissions, nominally only two and a half; but mounted to eight or ten at least, by the secret *manœuvres* of trade, not to include the advantage of purchasing goods wholesale, in common with contractors, and that of having so much money left in their hands—not to play with, I can assure you. Mushroom fortunes have started up during the war; the men, indeed, seem of the species of the fungus; and the insolent vulgarity which a sudden influx of wealth usually produces in common minds, is here very conspicuous, which contrasts with the distresses of many of the emigrants, "fallen—fallen from their high estate"[2] —such are the ups and downs of fortune's wheel! Many emigrants have met, with fortitude, such a total change of circumstances as scarcely can be paralleled, retiring from a palace, to an obscure lodging, with dignity; but the greater number glide about the ghosts of greatness,

---

2. John Dryden, "Alexander's Feast," lines 77–78.

with the *croix de St. Louis*[3] ostentatiously displayed, determined to hope, "though heaven and earth their wishes crossed." Still good-breeding points out the gentleman; and sentiments of honour and delicacy appear the offspring of greatness of soul, when compared with the grovelling views of the sordid accumulators of *cent. per cent.*[4]

Situation seems to be the mould in which men's characters are formed; so much so, inferring from what I have lately seen, that I mean not to be severe when I add, previously asking why priests are in general cunning, and statesmen false? that men entirely devoted to commerce never acquire, or lose, all taste and greatness of mind. An ostentatious display of wealth without elegance, and a greedy enjoyment of pleasure without sentiment, embrutes them till they term all virtue, of an heroic cast, romantic attempts at something above our nature; and anxiety about the welfare of others, a search after misery, in which we have no concern. But you will say that I am growing bitter, perhaps, personal. Ah! shall I whisper to you—that you—yourself, are strangely altered, since you have entered deeply into commerce—more than you are aware of—never allowing yourself to reflect, and keeping your mind, or rather passions, in a continual state of agitation—Nature has given you talents, which lie dormant, or are wasted in ignoble pursuits—You will rouse yourself, and shake off the vile dust that obscures you, or my

---

3. The issuance of this medal, established by Louis XIV in 1693 and conferred for military merit, had been discontinued in revolutionary France in 1792; hence it is a badge of the *ancien régime*, worn by the émigrés who hope for the reestablishment of the monarchy so that they can return home.

4. "Cent per cent." (usually written without two periods) is a return of interest equal to the principal; in short, complete profit.

understanding, as well as my heart, deceives me, egregiously—only tell me when? But to go farther a-field.

Madame La Fayette left Altona the day I arrived, to endeavour, at Vienna, to obtain the enlargement of her husband, or permission to share his prison.[5] She lived in a lodging up two pair of stairs, without a servant, her two daughters chearfully assisting; chusing, as well as herself, to descend to any thing before unnecessary obligations. During her prosperity, and consequent idleness, she did not, I am told, enjoy a good state of health, having a train of nervous complaints which, though they have not a name, unless the significant word *ennui* be borrowed, had an existence in the higher French circles; but adversity and virtuous exertions put these ills to flight, and dispossessed her of a devil, who deserves the appellation of legion.

Madame Genlis,[6] also, resided at Altona some time, under an assumed name, with many other sufferers of less note, though higher rank. It is, in fact, scarcely possible to stir out without meeting interesting countenances, every lineament of which tells you that they have seen better days.

At Hamburg, I was informed, a duke had entered into partnership with his cook, who becoming a *traiteur*, they were both comfortably supported by the

5. Adrienne Noailles, Marquise de La Fayette, was herself imprisoned for a time in France during the Revolution while her husband Gilbert was imprisoned in Austria, whence he fled to escape trial for treason. Allowed to leave France in 1795, she travelled to Hamburg, and then, with her two daughters, joined him in his prison in Olmütz, Austria, until the four were released in 1797. ("Enlargement" here means release from prison.)

6. Stéphanie-Felicité Ducrest de Sainte-Albin, Comtesse de Genlis, a French woman of letters and writer on education, had been governess to the Duke of Chartres' children.

profit arising from his industry. Many noble instances of the attachment of servants to their unfortunate masters, have come to my knowledge both here and in France, and touched my heart, the greatest delight of which is to discover human virtue.

At Altona, a president of one of the *ci-devant* parliaments keeps an ordinary, in the French style;[7] and his wife, with chearful dignity, submits to her fate, though she is arrived at an age when people seldom relinquish their prejudices. A girl who waits there brought a dozen *double louis d'or* concealed in her clothes, at the risk of her life, from France; which she preserves, lest sickness, or any other distress, should overtake her mistress, "who," she observed, "was not accustomed to hardships." This house was particularly recommended to me by an acquaintance of your's, the author of the American Farmer's Letters.[8] I generally dine in company with him: and the gentleman whom I have already mentioned, is often diverted by our declamations against commerce, when we compare notes respecting the characteristics of the Hamburgers. "Why, madam," said he to me one day, "you will not meet with a man who has any calf to his leg; body and soul, muscles and heart, are equally shrivelled up by a thirst of gain. There is nothing generous even in their youthful passions; profit is their only stimulus, and calculations the sole employment of their faculties; unless we except some gross animal gratifications which, snatched *at*

---

7. I.e., a former ("ci-devant") French nobleman keeps an eating place ("ordinary") that offers a fixed menu or *table d'hôte;* in the next sentence the girl who "waits" is thus a waitress.

8. Probably a reference to John Dickinson (1732–1808), whose series of "Farmer's Letters" in the *Pennsylvania Chronicle* in 1767 first gave form to the American colonial grievances.

spare moments, tend still more to debase the character, because, though touched by his tricking wand, they have all the arts, without the wit, of the wing-footed god."

Perhaps you may also think us too severe; but I must add, that the more I saw of the manners of Hamburg, the more was I confirmed in my opinion relative to the baleful effect of extensive speculations on the moral character. Men are strange machines; and their whole system of morality is in general held together by one grand principle, which loses its force the moment they allow themselves to break with impunity over the bounds which secured their self-respect. A man ceases to love humanity, and then individuals, as he advances in the chase after wealth; as one clashes with his interest, the other with his pleasures: to business, as it is termed, every thing must give way; nay, is sacrificed; and all the endearing charities of citizen, husband, father, brother, become empty names. But—but what? Why, to snap the chain of thought, I must say farewell. Cassandra was not the only prophetess whose warning voice has been disregarded. How much easier it is to meet with love in the world, than affection!

Your's, sincerely.

LETTER XXIV

MY LODGINGS at Altona are tolerably comfortable, though not in any proportion to the price I pay; but, owing to the present circumstances, all the necessaries of life are here extravagantly dear. Considering it as a temporary residence, the chief inconvenience of which, I am inclined to complain, is the rough streets that must be passed before Marguerite and the child can reach a level road.

The views of the Elbe, in the vicinity of the town, are pleasant, particularly as the prospects here afford so little variety. I attempted to descend, and walk close to the water edge; but there was no path; and the smell of glue, hanging to dry, an extensive manufactory of which is carried on close to the beach, I found extremely disagreeable. But to commerce every thing must give way; profit and profit are the only speculations—"double—double, toil and trouble."[1] I have seldom entered a shady walk without being soon obliged to turn aside to make room for the rope-makers; and the only tree, I have seen, that appeared to be planted by

---

1. *Macbeth*, IV.i.10.

the hand of taste, is in the church-yard, to shade the tomb of the poet Klopstock's wife.[2]

Most of the merchants have country houses to retire to, during the summer; and many of them are situated on the banks of the Elbe, where they have the pleasure of seeing the packet-boats arrive, the periods of most consequence to divide their week.

The moving picture, consisting of large vessels and small-craft, which are continually changing their position with the tide, renders this noble river, the vital stream of Hamburg, very interesting; and the windings have sometimes a very fine effect, two or three turns being visible, at once, intersecting the flat meadows: a sudden bend often increasing the magnitude of the river; and the silvery expanse, scarcely gliding, though bearing on its bosom so much treasure, looks for a moment, like a tranquil lake.

Nothing can be stronger than the contrast which this flat country and strand afford, compared with the mountains, and rocky coast, I have lately dwelt so much among. In fancy I return to a favourite spot, where I seemed to have retired from man and wretchedness; but the din of trade drags me back to all the care I left behind, when lost in sublime emotions. Rocks aspiring towards the heavens, and, as it were, shutting out sorrow, surrounded me, whilst peace appeared to steal along the lake to calm my bosom, modulating the wind that agitated the neighbouring poplars. Now I hear only an account of the tricks of trade, or listen to the distressful tale of some victim of ambition.

---

2. Friedrich Gottlieb Klopstock (1724–1803), German lyric poet, in 1754 married Margarethe Holler, the "Cidli" of his odes.

The hospitality of Hamburg is confined to Sunday invitations to the country houses I have mentioned, when dish after dish smoaks upon the board; and the conversation ever flowing in the muddy channel of business, it is not easy to obtain any appropriate information. Had I intended to remain here some time, or had my mind been more alive to general inquiries, I should have endeavoured to have been introduced to some characters, not so entirely immersed in commercial affairs; though, in this whirlpool of gain, it is not very easy to find any but the wretched or supercilious emigrants, who are not engaged in pursuits which, in my eyes, appear as dishonourable as gambling. The interests of nations are bartered by speculating merchants. My God! with what *sang froid* artful trains of corruption bring lucrative commissions into particular hands, disregarding the relative situation of different countries—and can much common honesty be expected in the discharge of trusts obtained by fraud? But this, *entre nous.*

During my present journey, and whilst residing in France, I have had an opportunity of peeping behind the scenes of what are vulgarly termed great affairs, only to discover the mean machinery which has directed many transactions of moment. The sword has been merciful, compared with the depredations made on human life by contractors, and by the swarm of locusts who have battened on the pestilence they spread abroad. These men, like the owners of negro ships, never smell on their money the blood by which it has been gained, but sleep quietly in their beds, terming such occupations *lawful callings;* yet the lightning marks not their roofs, to thunder conviction on them, "and to justify the ways of God to man."[3]

Why should I weep for myself? —"Take, O world! thy much indebted tear!"[4]

Adieu!

---

3. *Paradise Lost,* I.26.
4. This is obviously a quotation, but I have not been able to identify the source.

LETTER XXV

THERE is a pretty little French theatre at Altona; and the actors are much superiour to those I saw at Copenhagen. The theatres at Hamburg are not open yet, but will very shortly, when the shutting of the gates at seven o'clock forces the citizens to quit their country houses. But, respecting Hamburg, I shall not be able to obtain much more information, as I have determined to sail with the first fair wind for England.

The presence of the French army would have rendered my intended tour through Germany, in my way to Switzerland, almost impracticable, had not the advancing season obliged me to alter my plan. Besides, though Switzerland is the country which for several years I have been particularly desirous to visit, I do not feel inclined to ramble any farther this year; nay, I am weary of changing the scene, and quitting people and places the moment they begin to interest me. —This also is vanity!

DOVER

I left this letter unfinished, as I was hurried on board; and now I have only to tell you, that, at the sight of Dover cliffs, I wondered how any body could term them

them grand; they appear so insignificant to me, after those I had seen in Sweden and Norway.

Adieu! My spirit of observation seems to be fled—and I have been wandering round this dirty place, literally speaking, to kill time; though the thoughts, I would fain fly from, lie too close to my heart to be easily shook off, or even beguiled, by any employment, except that of preparing for my journey to London. —God bless you!

MARY_____

APPENDIX

PRIVATE business and cares have frequently so absorbed me, as to prevent my obtaining all the information, during this journey, which the novelty of the scenes would have afforded, had my attention been continually awake to inquiry. This insensibility to present objects I have often had occasion to lament, since I have been preparing these letters for the press; but, as a person of any thought naturally considers the history of a strange country to contrast the former with the present state of its manners, a conviction of the increasing knowledge and happiness of the kingdoms I passed through, was perpetually the result of my comparative reflections.

The poverty of the poor, in Sweden, renders the civilization very partial; and slavery has retarded the improvement of every class in Denmark; yet both are advancing; and the gigantic evils of despotism and anarchy have in a great measure vanished before the meliorating manners of Europe. Innumerable evils still remain, it is true, to afflict the humane investigator, and hurry the benevolent reformer into a labyrinth of errour, who aims at destroying prejudices quickly which only time can root out, as the public opinion becomes subject to reason.

An ardent affection for the human race makes enthusiastic characters eager to produce alteration in laws and governments prematurely. To render them useful and permanent, they must be the growth of each particular soil, and the gradual fruit of the ripening understanding of the nation, matured by time, not forced by an unnatural fermentation. And, to convince me that such a change is gaining ground, with accelerating pace, the view I have had of society, during my northern journey, would have been sufficient, had I not previously considered the grand causes which combine to carry mankind forward, and diminish the sum of human misery.

AUTHOR'S SUPPLEMENTARY NOTES

NOTE 1

NORWAY, according to geometrical measure, is 202 miles in length. In breadth it is very unequal. The common Norway mile contains about 24,000 yards, English measurement.

Norway is reckoned to contain 7558 quadrate miles: it is divided into four parts. There are four grand bailiffs, and four bishops. The four chief towns are Christiania, Thordhiem, Bergen, and Christiansand. Its natural products are wood, silver, copper, and iron, a little gold has been found, fish, marble, and the skins of several animals. The exportation exceeds the importation. The balance in favour of Norway, in the year 1767, was about 476,085 rixdollars, £95,217 sterling. It has been increasing ever since. The silver mines of Kongsberg yield silver to the amount of 350,000 rixdollars, £70,000 sterling; but it is asserted, that this sum is not sufficient to defray the expences of working them. Kongsberg is the only inland town, and contains 10,000 souls.

The copper mines at Rorraas yield about 4000 shippound a year; a ship-pound is 320 pounds: the yearly profit amounts to 150,000 rixdollars, £30,000 sterling. There are fifteen or sixteen iron works in Norway, which produce iron to the value of 400,000 rixdollars, £80,000 per annum.

The exportation of salted and dried fish is very considerable. In the year 1786 the returns for its exportation amounted to 749,200 rixdollars, £169,840.

There are four regiments of dragoons, each consisting of 108 men, officers included; two regiments of marching infantry, 1157 men each, with five companies in garrison, amounting to 3377 men; thirteen regiments of militia, 1916 men each, making 24,908 men; 960 men, light troops, who, in winter, whilst the snow is on the ground, run along on a kind of skates—a couple of long instruments made of wood.

NOTE 2

The Taxes in Norway consist of

1. A land tax. Farms, worth from two to three thousand dollars, pay from fifteen to twenty dollars annually.

2. A duty on all articles of provision, and on all goods carried in or out.

3. A tax on rank and office.

4. A tax on pensions and salaries; two per cent on one hundred dollars, and in proportion to ten per cent.

5. A tax on money put out to interest, with security on land or houses, of a quarter per cent. And as the allowed interest is four per cent the duty is one fourth of the interest.

ACKNOWLEDGMENTS

I want to thank Professors Stephen Hilliard, Frederick Link, Hugh Luke, James McShane, William C. Pratt, Paul Schach, and Desmond Wheeler for aiding me in identifying quotations and sources. I am grateful to Duane Roller and the staff at the DeGolyer Collection at the University of Oklahoma for aid in finding maps and illustrations; and to the University of Nebraska Library for the original edition which I used as my copy-text, to the Interlibrary Loan section for providing those books which were unavailable to me, and to Special Collections Librarian Robert Boyce for his aid and advice.

My excellent typist Peggy Briggs combines technical ability with a zeal for Wollstonecraft, and my competent proofreader Judy Wesely is an ardent feminist as well. Two other people have given that invaluable kind of support—spiritual aid. I thank Professor Gina Luria for being humane and scholarly in all she has done for me. And finally I thank my best friend, advisor, critic, and husband Larry Poston for loving and supporting me unfailingly in whatever I have attempted.

CAROL H. POSTON